Power Hands

An experiential guide to energy work

HELEN LEATHERS

Copyright Helen Leathers 2014
Helen Leathers asserts the moral right to be identified
as the authors of this work.

ISBN 978-0-9558571-9-5

A catalogue record for this book is available from the British Library.

First Published in 2014 by Spreading The Magic
www.spreadingthemagic.com

Cover Design by Titanium Design Ltd.
www.titaniumdesign.co.uk

All rights reserved. No part of this publication may be reproduced, stored in a retrieval system, or transmitted, in any form or by any means, electronic, mechanical, photocopying, recording or otherwise, without the prior permission of the publishers.

Please note that where it is indicated in the text that we are happy for copies of certain diagrams to be made for your personal use, the copyright remains ours and full credits must remain on each copy.

www.thepowerinyourhands.co.uk

The energy of the universe, the power, the magic that I speak of is not something elusive or external, it is not waiting to be 'found', harnessed or controlled. It simply is.

You do not need to earn the right, or prove yourself in order to embrace this energy. It is a part of who you are.

Rediscover the power and reconnect with yourself and your true essence.

It always is, and you always were.

CONTENTS

Introduction 1
  What is a Lightworker and Am I One?
  Working With The Light
  How to Use This Book

Understand The Power 7
 My Overview of The Universal Energy System
  My Overview of Our Energetic System
     - Auras
     - Chakras
     - Nadis
 How Does Energy Feel?
 Energetic Protection
 Power Points

Feel The Power 27
 Your Body & Your Breath
 Your Posture
 Your Hands
 Your Feet
 Your Centre
 Your Crown
 Bringing It All Together
 Energetic Protection
 Relaxation:
 Conscious Connection
 Opening
 Closing & Grounding

Use The Power 53
 Working With Your Energy Field
 Sensing Energy
 Healing
 Spiritual & Psychic Development
 Magic & Manifestation
 Be seen- or not!

CONTENTS (CONTINUED)

Other Things You Could Try 81
   Looking At Auras
        Dowsing The Chakras
        Psychometry
        Crystals

Personal Empowerment 87
        Improving Your Energy Levels
        Improving Your Life
        Be Powerful Beyond Measure

Appendices

Appendix A	Hand positions for a seated healing treatment	92
Appendix B	Hand positions for a healing treatment laying down	93
Appendix C	Chakras Guide	95
Appendix D	Body/chakras outline	97

Index Of Exercises & Visualisations

Protection Visualisation	24		Cleansing your Aura	54
Relaxation	28		Boost your Energy Levels	55
Breathing	29		Zipping Up	57
Tai Chi Exercises	30		Affecting Auras	58
Gassho	34		Scanning	60
Feel The Energy	34		Healing Energy	65
Feel The Aura	35		Group Healing	67
The Hand Game	35		Distance Healing Visualisation	69
Closing & Grounding	38		Harmonising Exercise	72
Centring	41		Working As An Energy Source	72
Crown Exercises	42		Be Seen	77
Bringing It All Together	43		Be Invisible	79
Conscious Connection	47		Looking At Auras	82
Elevating Your Energy	48		Dowsing The Chakras	82
Expanding Your Awareness	49		Psychometry	83

INTRODUCTION

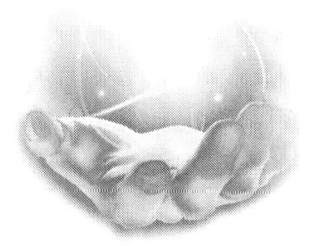

'Love the moment. Flowers grow out of the dark moments. Therefore each moment is vital. It affects the whole life. Life is a succession of moments and to live each, is to succeed."

Corita Kent (Artist & educator)

One evening, a few years ago, I was taking a look at an online forum about spiritual matters. Someone had posted a question asking how they could become a lightworker, one reply simply asked 'What's a lightworker?' That night I went to sleep but kept waking from the same repeating dream until I got up and started writing a reply to both questions. I put a short answer on the forum but that wasn't enough to let me go back to sleep. At 3a.m. there I was, pen in hand, and a book taking shape. This book is the result. It is an introduction to the basics of energy work that I hope will help many aspiring healers, and anyone interested in energy work, personal, spiritual or psychic development. You are all lightworkers.

It will also help guide those of you not yet on your path...but wondering. Maybe you can relate to this if you ever feel disconnected...from others, from life, or even from your own true nature. If you feel as though you're being swept along with the current, out of control and occasionally bumping your head on the odd rock. Are you envious of others who appear quite capable of plotting and navigating their course in life and who seem to have all the luck along the way? If you want to learn how to tap into the universal slipstream, pursue a more spiritual path in life, gain more of an understanding of energy or 'lightwork', learn to heal, channel or work with energy, or go down the road of psychic development work, then this book is for you.

In my mind there is little to beat the process of learning and acquiring new knowledge and skills; meeting others of a like-mind who are on a similar journey, finding the right teacher who you connect with and who can not only pass on the knowledge that you need but the inspiration, confidence and passion that will catapult you further along your chosen path. However, not everyone has the time, opportunity, funds or ability to find and attend relevant courses or workshops. Due to the personal nature of the type of work I'm writing about, some people may wish to keep their interest in the subject to themselves, at least at first.

By working through this book, together with practice, you'll start to feel more complete, more balanced, more energised and more connected with all of life. It will provide you with a platform from which to move into other areas of development, with an essential theoretical and practical understanding of the basics of energy work. This type of work is not for the chosen few but for everyone who wishes to pursue it. Neither does it have to be as complex as some would suggest. We're all a part of an energy system by the fact that we're alive, but when we consciously engage with it, that's when we can take things to another level.

I found that when I began to work with energy it changed my outlook on life and everything within it. It helped to explain so much for me and also allowed me to develop my existing skills and discover new ones. I believe that once you learn how energy work can be incorporated into your everyday life, you can really begin living to your full potential.

We only ever live in this moment right now and we can only ever change the moment in which we live. We can't change the past and the future is a result of the moments that lead up to it. Energy work creates a focus; it allows us to be more balanced, harmonious and happy now. And if we can achieve that now, in this moment, then we can achieve that for our future.

The information in this book is based on my work, teachings and experiences over the years. It's a simple straightforward system that will help you begin to develop spiritually on your own, or with others. It isn't the only way to learn about using universal energy, there are many other options available. I trust that if you've found this book, you were meant to find it and that it will be a good starting point for you. I hope that despite not working with you face-to-face, I can pass on not only the knowledge but also the inspiration, confidence and passion that I have for the subject and for your development.

INTRODUCTION

WHAT IS A LIGHTWORKER AND AM I ONE?

"When you make peace with yourself, you make peace with the world."

Maha Ghosananda
(Cambodian Buddhist monk & Nobel Peace Prize nominee)

Lightworkers are individuals who work with the energy of the universe for positive change. They seek to raise awareness and the spiritual consciousness of themselves, of others, and ultimately, of the planet.

I like the phrase 'lightworker' because the energy of the universe is just like a light. It can be increased in intensity or dulled into submission, but it's always there. Although it permeates everything, its nature is of a far higher vibrational level than the physical world we inhabit, so it never goes out, nor does it vanish at night. As we increase our awareness and work with the light for positive change, our vibration increases, our light gets brighter. When I think of lightworkers around the world, I have a vision of thousands of beacons of light, gradually turning up their intensity as they develop. The beauty of this is that lights illuminate the area around them, and eventually these individuals cannot help but affect others. This network of lights will eventually increase the light of the world, bringing more and more awareness of spiritual matters and our interconnectedness with others.

Those of us that are sensitive are more aware of the light and can sense it in others. It's brighter in those that work actively with it and those that are of a caring, open minded and spiritual nature, even if they're unaware of it. These are people in whose company we feel comfortable, relaxed, safe, accepted and nurtured. We are drawn to them and wish to spend time with them. They make us feel good about ourselves and about the world. In this way they're natural healers or lightworkers, whether they know it or not.

As lightworkers we each work in our own way, for the good of all, we may work alone or with others, or a combination of both and we all find a path that has meaning for us. No one person is insignificant, whatever your method of lightwork, it will all add to the overall global effect. You only need one spark to end darkness, so even if you only ever work on your own personal development, you're a lightworker. Ultimately we are only ever responsible for our own light, but we are able to create illumination for those around us.

WORKING WITH THE LIGHT

Tapping into the limitless source of universal energy can open many doors for us as we learn new skills and discover latent talents. Some of the benefits come about as a by-product of our connection through our own personal and spiritual development. For example; physical and mental relaxation, a level of detachment which can encourage a positive energy flow, release of negative thought patterns and cycles and an ability to overcome obstacles. You can use energy work to:

- Boost your own energy levels
- Keep your aura healthy, whole and protected
- Increase your intuition
- Increase your sensitivity
- Protect yourself from the negative effects of being too exposed to the energies and emotions of others
- Improve your meditation skills
- Get into the flow of life
- See your path in life
- Provide healing for yourself and others
- Improve your psychic abilities
- Increase your confidence
- Pave the way for future achievements
- Increase your chance of good fortune
- Help yourself deal with the 'stuff' of life
- Be seen - or not
- Work with magic and manifestation
- Undertake high-level energy work, such as 'rescue' and other advanced practises

Many people work with the light naturally but are unaware of certain fundamentals that can really help them to keep their feet on the ground, maintain their energy levels or work more efficiently or intensely. I will cover these basics in this book, along with methods that you can learn to make your progress faster and easier.

INTRODUCTION

HOW TO USE THIS BOOK

This book is divided into three main sections. The first, 'Understand The Power', gives you the background information, or theory behind energy work. This is based on various philosophies and schools of thought as well as my own experiences, thoughts and feelings that have helped me to create my own beliefs and understanding of the subject. It's a starting point for you, a frame of reference to enable you to move on to the practical work.

The second section, 'Feel The Power' is where you start to connect with and feel the energy. It works through each of the key elements that you will need to be aware of and work with including relaxation, breathing techniques, and how each area of the body relates to the whole system, before pulling everything together.

Section three, 'Use The Power' is full of exercises and ideas for connecting with and using universal energy.

Following the main sections, there are some other things you could try that will help you to be more efficient and increase the level of energy that you can work with. Then finally, there is a brief discussion to start you thinking about how this work can really empower you to have the life that you desire.

I recommend that you work through this book in stages and go over the practical work again and again. As with all work of this nature you don't read a book and wake up the next morning as a great healer or energy worker. The only way to really learn about the energy is to start to use it. You may wish to keep a diary or journal of what you do, when, and what your experiences and thoughts are and if they change as you develop. Persevere and, where possible, work with others to get feedback. Refer to the website www.thepowerinyourhands.co.uk for tools to help and guide you through the process, including micro-workshop videos, where you will be able to view some of the practical work that's described. Where a micro-workshop is available on the website a V will be shown next to the exercise. Many of the meditations and visualisation exercises are available as MP3 downloads (exercises will be marked with an A.) Full details of 'The Power In Your Hands Audio Collection' can be found at the website www.thepowerinyourhands.co.uk

Use this book as a map to discover your connection to everything. Eventually you may find that you want to join a group, healing course or something similar, to learn and practise some more.

Some other books and resources that may help you in your development can be found listed at the back of this book. Let yourself be guided to the work you like and are good at, or simply allow your new skills and understanding to help in the life you already lead. Most of all, enjoy. This is a lifelong process so take the pressure off yourself now and understand that it's the journey that's important, there isn't actually any destination.

Bright Blessings
Helen

UNDERSTAND THE POWER

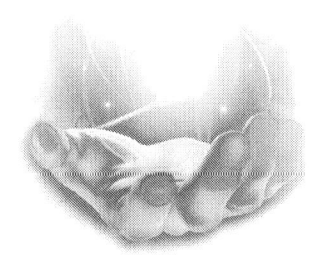

"A human being is a part of a whole, called by us a 'universe', a part limited in time and space. He experiences himself, his thoughts and feelings, as something separated from the rest... a kind of optical delusion of his consciousness. This delusion is a kind of prison for us, restricting us to our personal desires and to affection for a few persons nearest to us. Our task must be to free ourselves from this prison by widening our circle of compassion to embrace all living creatures and the whole of nature in its beauty."

Albert Einstein
(Theoretical physicist & Nobel Prize winner)

This is the background, or theory section of the book. It will help to create a framework within which to understand and work with energy and spiritual philosophy. Firstly, we need to consider the universe as an energetic system, and then ourselves as individual components of that system, and how we fit into, and interact with it. I will also explain how energy could feel to you and give you some extra tips that I've picked up along the way.

MY OVERVIEW OF THE UNIVERSAL ENERGY SYSTEM

In order to understand that we can utilise, affect and be affected by unseen energy, we need to look outside ourselves at the bigger picture and the part that we play within it. Most people consider themselves only as physical human beings, which is fair enough, given that that's how we appear. However, some of us come to question this throughout life, often as a result of personal experiences, and subsequently to feel or realise that we are far more than just our bodies. What I describe here is my take on the universal energy system as a whole, and may take time to understand. While I do try to keep it as simple as possible, you may need to re-read this section a few times. It also has to sit comfortably within your belief system. If it doesn't, but it enables you to formulate your own thoughts about what you believe and how you see this reality, then that's great. That's what I want you to do.

When I talk about energy or light work I am referring to consciously working with the 'vital life force' that animates all living things. This 'life force energy' has many different names from many different cultures; ki, prana, chi, mana, some will call it god, love, divine source - the list is virtually endless. Essentially everything is energy. All matter vibrates at different rates depending on what it is. Take, for example water. Slow down the vibratory rate of its molecules, through cooling, and it becomes ice. Speed it up, by heating, and it becomes steam.

My belief is that we are all a part of a bigger 'structure' that exists on many levels. I will call this structure 'the divine source' or simply 'the divine', for want of a non-denominational term. You can call it whatever you feel comfortable with; 'God', 'Goddess', 'original source' - it's all the same to me.

Connecting all of us as 'parts' to each other and helping to form this bigger structure is the essence or 'life force energy'. This energy runs through us all on an invisible, higher vibrational level through a system of subtle energy channels in much the same way as blood runs through our veins on the physical level.

If the divine source is omnipresent, all encompassing, it must be within and without of each of us; a part of us as much as we are a part of it. How can we possibly begin to comprehend this? Here is an analogy that may help:

Imagine if you will, a large mass of water, not contained within anything, invisible, just 'there'. You cannot always see it, but all of the molecules that make up this body of water have an effect on each other. Think of the spreading nature of ripples and waves. Imagine that something tiny is dropped in at certain points within this body of water, a chemical substance that causes the water in the immediate vicinity to clump together forming a gel-like mass. It's more concentrated, more solid and more visible in these places. It's still the same original water, in essence, still connected to and within the larger mass of water, still a part of it, affected by it, effective on it, but at first glance something quite different and apart from it.

Let's suggest that there are many points like this within the body of water and that they're able to move around independently. As they move, they cause ripples and waves affecting the body of water surrounding them and to a greater or lesser degree the other gel-like structures within it. Movement and changes within the rest of the body of water would affect them too, however imperceptibly. Each structure has a relationship through this interconnectedness, with each other and with the body of water itself.

In this analogy, the body of water represents the divine source, the chemical drops are a seed of individual consciousness, creating living individual beings and things (the gel-like structure).

Do you see how, using this analogy, we as individuals living within the divine source are a part of the whole and affect every other individual and the energy around us, and that they also affect us?

In an energetic system energy can't be created or destroyed - it can only change form. Therefore we must all have been a part of the original divine source. Neale Donald Walsch really helps to explain this concept in his 'Conversations with God' series of books (that I strongly recommend). He suggests that 'God' did not know how wonderful and creative s/he was until s/he had created something wonderful. He also explains how each of us must experience being *apart from* 'God', in order to appreciate being *a part of* 'God'. How can you appreciate what you are in the absence of anything to compare with? For example, you would not say you were tall if everyone that you'd ever met was also 6'5". It's all relative. So the divine creates individual objects and beings that are in essence, a part of itself, made from the divine source, because there is nothing else with which to compare or to help understanding its true creative nature.

> *"Relativity teaches us the connection between the different descriptions of one and the same reality."*
>
> Albert Einstein

To become a lightworker we must be able to connect with, tap into and consciously channel the divine energy within and without of us. You don't have to live in a commune or be a monk or a hermit, to do this. I believe that we are here in human form to experience just that, being in physical, human form. However, we also have to remember who we truly are in essence, a part of the divine, and then learn to integrate these two elements; our physical and spiritual sides, in order to practically and physically experience our divine creative nature and our interconnectivity.

So, as energy workers, if we can tune into the energy of the divine source and connect with its flow, we can come into harmony with our original state of being, and help others to do the same. Being in harmony, or not can feel as different as desperately swimming against a rip tide or gently floating with the stream.

MY OVERVIEW OF OUR OWN ENERGY SYSTEM

By understanding our own energy system, how it sits within, links us to and interacts with the bigger energetic structure, the 'divine source', we can learn how to consciously work with and channel energy for a more positive and fulfilling life experience. There are many theories about the way in which universal energy flows through us individually, none of which can currently be completely proven by scientific means. My overview is based on esoteric teachings and my experience of working as a healer and complementary therapist, as well as in psychic development circles. It's what has felt right and worked for me in all of my work.

Our energetic systems consist of – auras, chakras and nadis.

Auras
In Eastern and esoteric teachings it's said that we exist on many levels. These levels are like overlapping layers of ourselves, taking up the same space but each at a progressively higher vibratory rate. Our physical body has the slowest vibratory rate (imagine it as ice), making us solid, present in the physical world and therefore visible to others. Overlying our physical body are the etheric, emotional (or astral), mental and spiritual bodies (imagine them as steam). Because of their higher vibratory rates, these are not visible to most people, although some people can pick them up through sensing, feeling or seeing the energy given off by them. These emanations are termed as the 'aura' and each energetic body has its own. They are three-dimensional, extending out around, above and below the body. Auras could be likened to the electro-magnetic field that emanates from an atomic structure.

From lowest to highest vibratory frequency these energy bodies are:
- Etheric Body: resembles the physical body in shape and dimension; it draws in vital energy, stores it and distributes it to the physical and other subtle bodies through the chakras and nadis (covered later). The aura of this body extends for about 5cm and is the same shape as the body.
- Emotional or Astral Body: occupies about the same space as the physical body; it carries feelings, emotions and character traits that are transmitted by its aura and can sometimes be seen as colours. The aura is oval in shape and may extend from a few centimetres up to several metres around a person.
- Mental Body: oval in shape, this body can increase in volume taking up as much space as the astral body and its aura combined. Its main function is to assimilate information about universal truths provided by the spiritual body and integrate them with the rational conscious mind. The aura of this body extends for several metres.
- Spiritual or Causal Body: oval in shape. The aura of this body can extend from one metre to several miles around the physical body and changes from an oval to a perfect circle. This body receives information and energy from the spiritual plane of being and passes it down to the lower bodies.

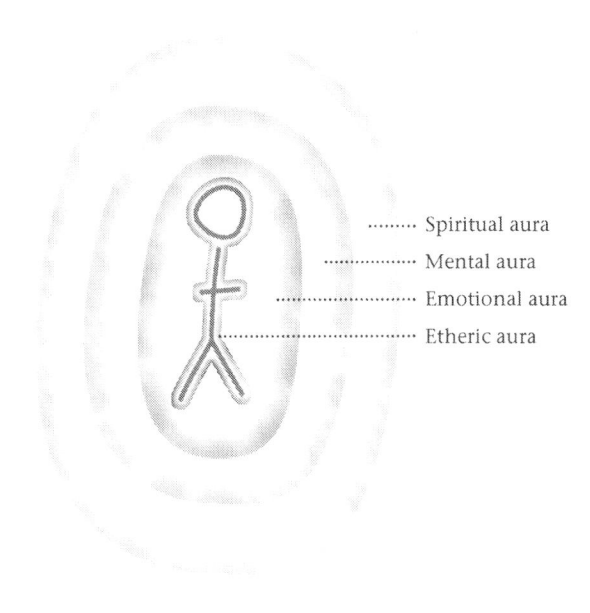

Chakras

There are seven major chakras, forming a column down the centre of the body, in line with the spine. They are points of concentrated energy within the aura that form wheels of energy extending out, like funnels, usually to the front and back of us. The chakras take in energy from the universe then transform it into a lower frequency, to be redistributed throughout our energy system. Eastern philosophies teach that, in order for us to be whole, healthy, creative, and to continue to develop spiritually, our chakras must be working in harmony with each other, allowing a positive, steady flow of energy. Each of the main chakras contain all colour vibrations but one colour always dominates. This colour corresponds to the primary task of the chakra.

The chakras are always 'open' but to varying degrees. They can be too open or for others, less open, causing a restricted energy flow. If the energy flow is out of balance it can be indicative of an imbalance in certain parts of our lifestyle, health, emotions or thinking.

There are also many smaller chakras including those in the palms of our hands; used particularly when giving healing, and in the soles of the feet; useful to visualise when grounding our energies. (More on these later.)

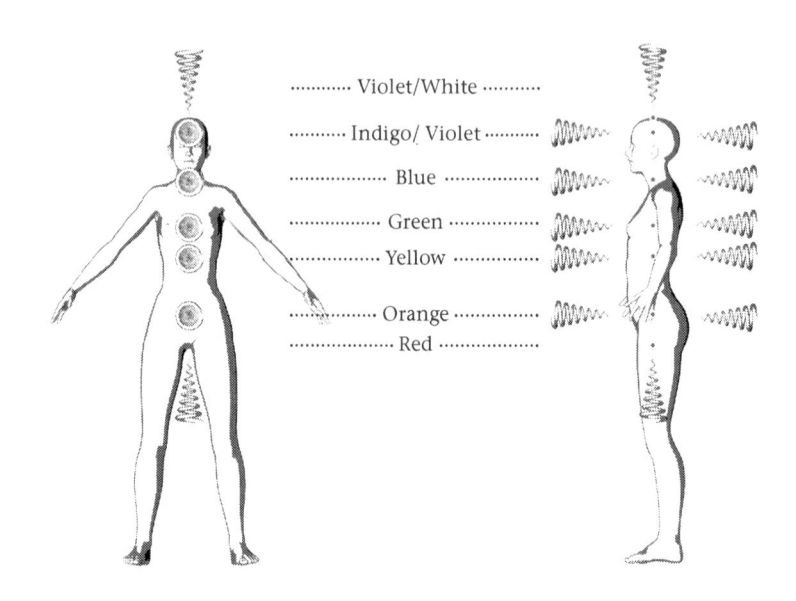

Violet/White
Indigo/Violet
Blue
Green
Yellow
Orange
Red

The Seven Main Chakras:

Base Chakra - Red
Located at the perineum, this chakra opens downwards. It connects us to the physical world, keeps us grounded and is said to be the seat of the collective unconscious. If this chakra is too open we may be overly concerned with material things, possibly self-indulgent. If this chakra is too closed we may be run down physically, have a tendency to worry too much, or feel 'away with the fairies'. Grounding work would be important to keep our feet on the ground.

Sacral Chakra - Orange
Located two fingers below the navel. It's related to our primordial emotions, security, sexuality, empowerment and creativity. If this chakra is too open we may crave a more meaningful relationship, not realising that the most important one is with ourselves. We may need to be more embracing of the miracles of nature. If this chakra is too closed we may withdraw from the attention or sensual signals from others, life may seem a bit boring, we may need to learn to express our feelings.

Solar Plexus Chakra - Yellow
Located at the diaphragm, this chakra is our power centre. It connects us to the astral body and helps us to perceive the vibrations of others. If this chakra is too open, we may be too open to the energies of others and need to learn to protect ourselves. (Folding our arms over this area if feeling uncomfortable can help prevent us from picking up negativity from others or our surroundings) If this chakra is too closed, we may be insensitive to others' energy or to our surroundings. We may need to learn to extend our awareness and be more observant.

Heart Chakra - Green (sometimes pink)
Said to be the seat of unconditional love. This chakra is related to healing, empathy and sympathy. It connects us to the spiritual aspect of others and ourselves. If this chakra is too open it's possibly as a result of constantly putting others before ourselves. A closed down heart chakra is often found in those who do not like themselves, or find it difficult to trust or love others. We may need to learn to be kinder to and forgive ourselves.

Throat Chakra - Blue
This chakra relates to expression, communication (including listening) and inspiration. It connects us with the mental body. An overly open throat chakra is common among public speakers, or those who feel driven to communicate continually for whatever reason. A closed down throat chakra is found if we are unable to communicate our feelings with others, if we don't listen to others or fail to notice signs around us.

Third Eye or Brow Chakra – Indigo or violet
Located slightly above and between the eyes. This chakra relates to psychic perception and intuition. It's said to connect us to all levels of creation. If this chakra is too open we may be too focused on intellect and reason, try to rationalise everything and influence the thoughts of others. If this chakra is too closed we may only accept what we can actually see, be forgetful or lose our head in a crisis. In either case we may benefit from developing our intuitive and psychic side.

Crown Chakra - Violet or white
Located on the crown of the head, this chakra opens upwards. It's related to universal knowledge and connects us to the spiritual plane. The crown chakra becomes more open with spiritual advancement. It cannot be too open. The crown is always connecting us to spirit, however, if it appears small or narrow, you may wish to actively pursue a more spiritual path.

Nadis
Energy is carried through the aura and to and from the chakras by a system of vessels, much like the veins and arteries that carry blood around the physical body. In Indian and Tibetan teachings these are called nadis. The most significant of these channels are the main central channels; sushumna, ida and pingala.

The sushumna follows the line of the spinal column and connects all the chakras from base to crown. Ida and pingala run either side of sushumna and some writings say that they entwine around the sushumna. These vessels are said to extract the vital energy from the air that we breathe and dispose of any toxic energies through our exhalations. Ida begins on our right hand side, just below the base chakra and finishes up at our right nostril. Pingala begins on our left hand side, just below the base chakra and ends at our left nostril.

UNDERSTAND THE POWER

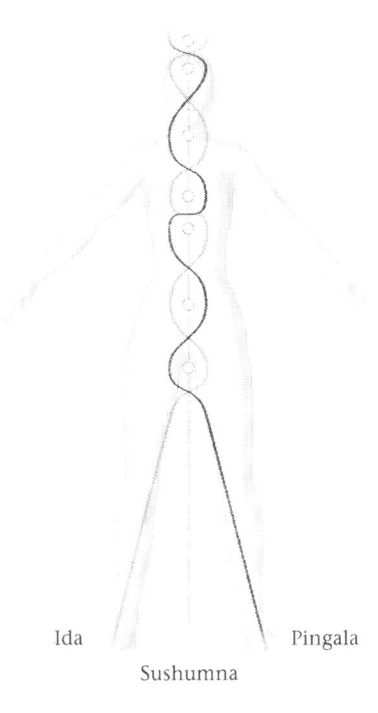

Ida   Pingala
Sushumna

Can you see the similarity between the pattern made by the main energy channels and the symbol known as the caduceus (below)? Caduceus has become the symbol associated with medicine and healing and I don't believe that's a coincidence.

It's believed that heavenly ki (the universal energy representing the 'male' aspect of the divine) enters your energy system through the crown chakra and earthly ki (the universal energy representing the female aspect of the divine) enters through the base chakra. Original ki (the energy that is instilled in us at the moment of our conception) is stored in our 'sacral centre'. This place is in the centre of our abdomen just below our navel, that we may understand in the west as our 'centre of gravity'.

In India one of the disciplines of moving energy through the energy channels is called 'raising the kundalini' and its major goal is spiritual growth. It's said that unawakened, female, kundalini energy rests like a coiled serpent at the base of the spine. When she is awakened by our growing consciousness, she rises and moves up along the sushumna or central channel, activating the chakras, increasing our spiritual evolution or development, to unite eventually with the heavenly, male energy or Shiva at the crown chakra. The union is described as a state of bliss and the fusion of heaven and earth.

In China and Japan they have a slightly different slant on energy work and I will share this briefly with you for a couple of reasons. Firstly because this may be your frame of reference as you may have come across it in other disciplines such as tai chi or shiatsu, and secondly because it may work better for you. It's best if you can choose a system of understanding and practice that works for you and allows you to develop, rather than attempt to go along with something that doesn't quite sit right with you, as this will only block your development.

The energy vessels in Chinese and Japanese culture are known as meridians and are the basis for disciplines such as shiatsu and acupuncture. The most prominent of these are called the conception vessel and governing vessel. Both are said to originate from the tan tien (similar to the 'sacral centre' as described above) and follow a line down to the perineum (base chakra area). From here the conception vessel runs up the front midline of the body to the mouth, entering and travelling down inside the body to the kidneys and uterus (in women). The governing vessel travels up the spine at the back of the body, over the head and down the centreline of the face to the mouth, where it meets up with the conception vessel and continues the same journey inside.

In China and Japan the energetic practises equivalent to those in India and Tibet are known as 'chi kung' or 'qi gong' and their main goal is replenishing life force energy and therefore maintaining good health and ensuring a long life. In this practise the energy or prana is moved in a circular pathway. The subject connects with the energy at the tan tien, sinks it down to the perineum, up the governing vessel along the line of the spine and over the head to the mouth and the down along the front midline of the body through the conception vessel, continuing this circuit of energy or 'microcosmic orbit' as it's known.

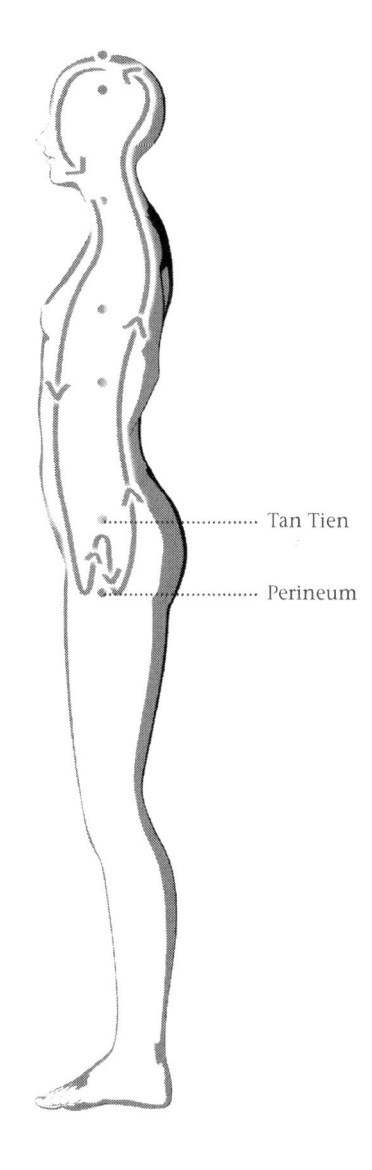

.... Tan Tien

.... Perineum

I believe that we are naturally connected to and channel universal energy through our energetic system by the very fact that we are alive. We also take it in through the air, food and drink as well as via our own energetic system. But when we want to *consciously* tap into and channel energy we need to have more of an understanding of how it all works. This helps us to visualise what we're doing and to feel, alter and direct the energy flow. This understanding and awareness gives us even more access to the energy of the universe.

From my experience as a Reiki Master I believe that Reiki is one discipline that allows this conscious channelling. Energy is drawn in through the crown chakra, along the main central channels and along branches of meridians or nadis to the hands. The Reiki attunements open and clear the central channels, increasing the flow and facilitating the conscious element of the process. They also allow us to learn to fine tune and adapt the energy and to increase the amount and strength of it. Each level of the Reiki process takes us further in our abilities, and along our journey of development and understanding. Although a particular system of learning will give you guidelines to work to I don't think that you necessarily need to follow any one discipline. It's quite possible to become a lightworker without 'official' training. (However, you still need to practise and discover how it works for you.)

By learning to control the energy flow you can become adept at storing and transmitting the energy. By working to expand your energy channels, you can increase your ability as a lightworker. The exercises and ideas in this book can help you to do exactly this.

HOW DOES ENERGY FEEL?

When we work with universal energy we can experience many different sensations and each of us can feel it in different ways. So, although it's interesting to share your experiences, please don't compare them, as there's no right or wrong way to feel the energy. Equally, when working with others, don't be at all surprised if they 'feel' the energy differently to you, even if they're receiving healing energy from you.

When you start to consciously work with energy you'll probably be as fascinated as I was with the physical sensations that you experience. I remember very clearly sensing my own energy flowing through me for the first time. I was having a reflexology treatment with someone who, it turns out, was a very wonderful healer.

UNDERSTAND THE POWER

As she worked on my feet I felt the energy flowing and buzzing - it was like vibrant bubbling spring water running all through my veins and it was amazing.

Common sensations are heat, cold, tingling, bubbling, buzzing, fizziness, a sense of flowing movement, lightness, heaviness in all or parts of your body, a sense of weightlessness, particularly in your arms.

Sensing energy directly, either within you or through your contact with a person or object, can be very different to feeling its fluctuations around you, or sensing energy emanating from other people. For example, I am sure most of us have met someone who we feel really drawn to or conversely, somebody that we don't like standing too close to for some inexplicable reason. This is one way in which we sense the person's energy or aura. It doesn't mean that they're a good or bad person, just that your energies either complement each other or not. This is a very simplified diagram to illustrate the point.

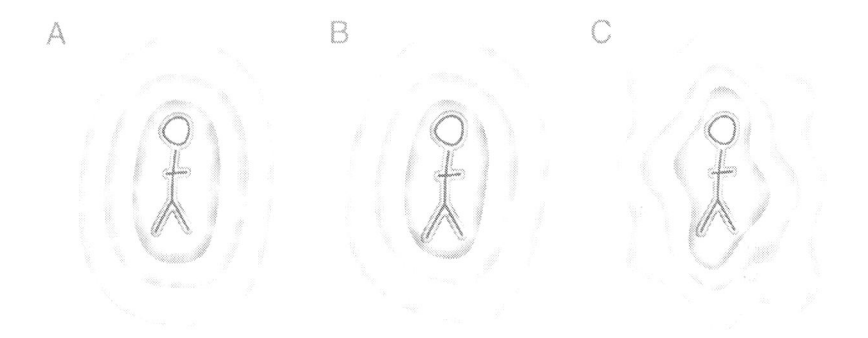

A   B   C

Imagine that you are person 'B'. You will probably find that A's energy resonates with yours, you are both comfortable in and enjoy each others company. Whereas C's energy is more 'spikey', so you may feel uncomfortable in their presence.

We can also pick up on energies from our surroundings, particularly if there's paranormal activity. Have you ever walked into a room and felt uneasy, or simply known that friends have just had a row? How would you know, unless you were sensitive to an altered, uncomfortable energy around the place or person?

Sensing these external energy changes can make you feel hot or cold, slightly dizzy or even nauseous. You may feel it in your solar plexus area, almost like nervousness or 'butterflies', or you might just know things intuitively.

I occasionally get a feeling of 'too much' energy within or around me. This can make me feel really hot, fidgety or anxious, or sometimes I get an uncomfortable feeling as though I have eaten far too much and don't know what to do with myself.

Another way that we sense energy is to suddenly feel an emotion that isn't our own, quite out of the blue. If this happens you are more than likely picking this up from someone near to you, or possibly from residual energy imprinted on a location by an event in the past.

When you become used to sensing energy you may find that you are skilled at picking up on certain types of energy, for example, spirit presences, earth energy or ley lines, or auric energy. With practise you will learn to differentiate between and interpret them all.

ENERGETIC PROTECTION

Before you begin any sort of energy work, it's essential to understand the need for protection, what it means, and how to put it in place. Psychic or energetic protection is anything that strengthens your aura and creates a safe place around you that nothing negative can penetrate. It keeps the aura from being depleted, damaged or affected by negative energies or entities. Think of it in the same way as keeping physically healthy: boosting your immune system to prevent yourself from catching bugs that may be going around, and eating well and exercising to maintain physical health and optimum energy.

Please understand that integrating a conscious awareness of and connection to universal energy does not mean that you need to put protective barriers up all the time. Also, channelling healing energy for yourself or others does not deplete your energy and I rarely use 'full on' protective measures when simply giving healing. However, if you decide to go down the route of connecting with spirit or developing your psychic abilities, it's essential to put protection in place every time that you start to work in this way. The reason for this is that when we work we raise our vibratory rate. We refer to this as our 'light'. It's almost as if we are turning up a dimmer switch, making us more noticeable to those who can see or sense it. Spirit beings are attracted to this light. Generally they are benevolent spirits who visit to offer their wisdom, messages of love and support or information to those they have left behind. However it's also possible to attract mischievous or even, in the worst-case scenario, malevolent spirits. This is rare and easily prevented simply by staying positive and not dwelling on anything even remotely negative. Be aware of these very rare possibilities, put protective measures in place before you begin and then forget about them and maintain a positive working environment throughout. There is a wonderful Native American saying that says it all, 'Keep your face to the sunlight and you will not see the shadows.' Basically you will attract what you focus on so always work with positive thoughts.

It's far more likely that you'll need to protect your energy from more mundane everyday things and people. This is because you will become more sensitive to the needs, emotions and energies of others as you develop your intuitive skills. Sensing the emotions of others can be overpowering and wearing. It's also difficult, especially in the early days to differentiate between others' feelings and your own, so you need to use protective measures to ensure that there are boundaries in place. You will find that people (and animals) are drawn to your 'light'. This will include like-minded people as well as individuals who may need help. It's usually subconscious, but they somehow know that you can help them or give them something that they lack, such as healing energy, confidence or a more positive outlook. Although this can be flattering you do have to be careful as it's easy to want to help everyone and that can take a toll on you. Again, you must be careful that you have boundaries in place ensuring you don't just give to others all the time without worrying about yourself. Remember also that there's a fine line between helping someone and them becoming dependent on you. Ultimately, you cannot be responsible for anyone other than yourself.

Examples of when you may need to use protection are listed here as a guide:
- If your energy levels are low, you feel negative or unhappy, especially for no particular reason.
- If you feel that you're giving too much of yourself to others or that others may be taking advantage of your good nature.
- If you feel vulnerable or uncomfortable.
- If you're around anyone who are focussing on negative subjects and you're unable to change the conversation to more positive matters, or escape their company.
- If you suspect that someone is being angry, resentful or negative towards you.
- Any time that your intuition is telling you that you should.
- When connecting with spirit or practising psychic development techniques (You can find out more about these from The Spiritual & Psychic Development Workbook, see page 104)

There are many ways of protecting yourself, some of which are listed below. Try them out and choose the one that you feel most comfortable and confident with. You can also use a combination of any number of them.

Visualisation
Imagine some form of protective shield around you and your aura. This could be a force field of bright white light, a bubble, an egg, mirrors reflecting away from you or you could see yourself inside a hollow crystal filled with light. Know that you're safe, completely sealed in and protected from outside influences. I always visualise a circle of light blue flames, like a gas burner on a hob, around myself, or the group I'm working with. They are safe for us but keep out any negative energy. Here's an example of a protection visualisation for you to practise with:

Protection Visualisation:
When you feel that you need to protect your energies perform the following exercise:
- Visualise your aura around you as though it is a giant egg shape and you are inside it.
- See it as being filled with pure white light.
- Now imagine that the outside edge hardens like a shell around your egg, and turns to metallic silver reflecting any negative intentions or energy that comes your way.
- Know that nothing can get in or out.

As you practise and become adept at visualisation you may be able to give yourself a trigger word that will allow this state of protection to be created instantaneously. It may be 'protect', 'shields up' or something similar. Don't use this everyday as it's a powerful visualisation, only use it when you need it. In general daily activities knowing that your spirit guides, angels and loved ones in spirit are around you and can offer protection, should be more than sufficient.

Talisman
Wearing a crystal or symbol can act as protection. Look into it in detail and find something appropriate and comfortable for you. For some it could be a religious symbol, or an item given to them by a loved one. The best crystal I have found for protection is Black Tourmaline. I also use a pentagram*, which is an ancient pro-

tective symbol and occasionally, if I feel drawn to it, a rosary made from haematite (another stone with protective qualities). I believe that these talismans or symbols work for a number of reasons. Firstly because you believe that they will, and secondly because of countless others throughout time who have had the same belief, therefore imbuing the symbol with a protective essence. These items should all be cleansed before use and at regular intervals (perhaps monthly) during prolonged use to help expel anything unwanted that they absorb while they are protecting your energies. One of the simplest methods of doing this is to allow the item to sit in a pot of salt over night. (Do dispose of the salt afterwards though.) Or you can leave them for a few days in direct sunlight or moonlight, especially at a full moon.

*The pentagram is a 5 pointed star and represents many things including the interconnection of the five elements; air, water, earth, fire and spirit.

Physical
Crossing your legs at the ankles and your arms at the wrists seals your energy circuit not allowing others to tap into it. In some cases, you probably do this automatically. You've probably been aware of folding your arms across yourself when you're uncomfortable with someone or perhaps disagree with them. This also works to contain your energy and prevent it from being sapped by others.

Ask
Before beginning any psychic or spiritual development work or if you ever feel uneasy or in need of some psychic protection, ask your spirit guides, angels or loved ones in spirit to draw close to you and keep you safe and protected. The following 'Protection Request' will prepare you for undertaking a meditation, psychic reading and any other exercise detailed in this book. If you suffer from dis-

turbed sleep or bad dreams, you can use the beginning of this protection request (in bold) before going to sleep at night or at any time that you feel the need for extra support or protection. While saying it you can also visualise a bubble of white protective light all around your room or yourself.

Protection Request:
- Take a moment to close your eyes and calm your mind.
- Concentrate on your breathing, allowing the breath to become deeper and slower.
- Mentally ask your spirit guides and angels to draw close and offer their assistance using the following script:

"**I call upon my spirit guides, angels and loved ones in spirit to draw close to me and to create a circle of protection around me ensuring that I am safe and protected at all times and on all levels. I ask for your protection, guidance and wisdom** while I work and afterwards. I am happy to work with guidance from the spirit world and to communicate with them, but I do so only in love and light and with the highest intentions. I ask that anyone from the spirit world who wishes to assist or communicate does so with the same intentions, and that my Guides and angels enforce this on my behalf."

Ongoing Maintenance
To ensure that you're working at your optimum, and are able to deal with any situations that may require protection, overall wellbeing is essential. Keep your own energy levels up, keep healthy and positive, have or give yourself healing regularly, take exercise, work on strengthening your aura and practise visualisations. Also ensure that you take time to rest and enjoy yourself.

Be aware of your own negative thoughts and actions and the effects they could have on yourself and others. If you realise that you're having negative thoughts or feelings, change what you're thinking about or focussing on. Try to do something more positive, or find a positive aspect in the situation. Daily positive affirmations are an excellent way of countering any negative 'self talk'. Maybe you've never realised that you do this but most of us have some kind of negative programming in our brain that we would be better off getting rid of. 'I'm too fat, too thin, not good enough, too lazy, too stupid.' What does your 'self talk' tell you? What would you rather hear about yourself? Create a simple counter affirmation and use it regularly.

UNDERSTAND THE POWER

Write it out and stick it on your mirror so that you see it every day. If you can't think of one, simply use 'I am perfect'. Or download your free 'I Am Mirror' from the 'Readers Resources' at www.spreadingthemagic.com.

POWER POINTS

Some important points I would like to share with you before you start working with energy.

- Don't undertake energy work too soon after you've eaten as your energies need to be working on the physical level for digestion. If you begin to raise your energy vibration above the physical level it can make you feel very uncomfortable and possibly a bit sick or light-headed. Take my word for it, it's not a nice feeling!
- Never undertake energy work after alcohol or any recreational drugs. This is non-negotiable as far as I'm concerned. Your inhibitions and defences will be lower and you will be more vulnerable to possible negative energies or experiences. Working with energy on higher levels enters us into an altered state of consciousness in itself and creates its own positive 'high' without any negative side effects.
- Remember: To ensure you do not run the risk of having a bad experience when working energetically always put protection in place before you begin, maintain a positive atmosphere while working and close down and ground your energies at the end of the session (see page 38)
- Only work with people you feel comfortable with, and teachers that you have confidence in. There is a Wiccan proviso for working in a circle or coven, 'In perfect love and perfect trust', I believe that this should hold true for all forms of development work no matter what the creed associated with it.
- At some points in this book I do talk about communication with spirit, however, I appreciate that this may be a cause of concern for some people. The golden rule is always to work with positive and highest intentions. Spirit should never hurt you or encourage you to do anything harmful to yourself or others or to act inappropriately. If at any time you're at all concerned by your experiences you should seek help from an experienced and reputable medium, healer, or if necessary, a medical practitioner.

FEEL THE POWER

"The flower draws its life energy from the soil and from the sun. We are very similar. We continuously receive energy from the earth through our feet and from the air. Energy is everywhere, like love. We just have to open ourselves up to receive it."

Ratu Bagus
(Healer and spiritual teacher)

Here I will show you how to get to grips with the practicalities, stage by stage, and start to feel the energy and learn to work with it. Beginning with relaxation, breathing techniques and getting your posture right, before working through the key areas of the body and how they relate to energy work. And finally how to pull it all together and how all the elements work in combination. People learn in a variety of different ways, so you will find tools such as micro-workshop videos available at www.thepowerinyourhands.co.uk which will fit in with the exercises described here. So, if you're unsure of any of my descriptions, take a look. As you go through the exercises in this section observe and make note of any sensations you experience and how they change as you become more attuned to and aware of the energy flowing through you. Typically the hands are the easiest place to 'feel' the energy as this is where we are used to 'feeling' or 'touching'. However, this can take time, so be patient.

YOUR BODY & YOUR BREATH

It's very difficult to focus on energy work, which is of a 'higher' nature if you're caught up with thoughts of a more earthly nature. Perhaps you have physical aches, pain, tension or discomfort, or maybe your mind is worrying over everyday stuff. So before we begin any practical work with the more subtle energy system we must be aware of and be able to relax the physical body. We can also use the process of breathing to help with physical and mental relaxation and to slow the activity of the mind, encouraging a meditative state. Eventually you'll do these exercises naturally without thinking about them, although you may find on occasion it's useful for you to go through them consciously once more to ensure complete relaxation.

Exercise 1 - Simple Tension & Relaxation Exercise <u>A</u>
You can lie down if you wish, but if you're tired this can encourage sleep. It's best to sit upright in a chair, or cross-legged on the floor, supported by a cushion if required.

Simply take your attention to each area of your body in turn. Slowly and systematically focus your attention on each muscle group, tensing and holding it for a few seconds and then consciously releasing it.

Take your time and don't rush through - you may want to repeat this exercise a second time for a deeper relaxation.

- Sit or lie comfortably.
- Take your awareness to your hands, make a tight fist, hold for a count of three and release.
- Tense your lower arms, hold for three, and release.
- Tense your upper arms, hold for three, and release.
- Tense your shoulders, lifting them up towards your ears, hold for three, and release.
- Take your awareness to your neck: pull your chin down towards your chest but keep it from touching chest, hold for three and then release.
- Take your awareness to your lower face and jaw, bite hard and pull back the corners of your mouth hold for three and then release.
- Now, open your mouth wide as though you are yawning, hold for 3, then release.
- Screw your eyes up and wrinkle your nose, hold for three and then release.
- Move your awareness to your forehead, lift your eyebrows as high as possible, hold for three and then release.
- Take your awareness to your upper torso, pull your shoulder blades together hold for three and then release.

- Tense your stomach muscles, pulling your bellybutton in towards your spine, hold for three and then release.
- Taking your awareness to your legs tense your thigh muscles, hold for three and then release.
- Pull your toes towards your head tensing your calf muscles hold for three and then release.
- Taking your awareness to your feet, point and curl toes downwards, hold for three and then release.
- Tense your whole body at once, hands, arms, face, neck, chest, stomach, thighs, calves and feet, screw your eyes up, hold for three, two, one, and completely release.
- *(Move straight on to the next stage.)*

Exercise 2 - Breathing Exercise <u>A</u>
- Take your awareness to your breathing, preferably through your nose, as this is more relaxing.
- Ensure that you are breathing slowly and deeply.
- As you inhale, your abdomen will gently rise. And as you exhale it will fall.
- If your mind drifts or you lose track during this exercise bring your attention back to refocus on your breathing.
- Take a long, slow, deep inhalation for a count of 1 - 2 - 3 - 4, hold for 1- 2 and exhale for 1 - 2 - 3 - 4.
- In 2 3 4, Hold *(pause)*, Out 2 3 4
- In 2 3 4, Hold *(pause)*, Out 2 3 4
- In 2 3 4, Hold *(pause)*, Out 2 3 4
- In 2 3 4, Hold *(pause)*, Out 2 3 4
- In 2 3 4, Hold *(pause)*, Out 2 3 4
- Continue breathing slowly and deeply until you're ready to move on to the next stage. It's not a race or a competition, just a way of relaxing and focusing your mind on the moment.
- You can start to lengthen the breath once you're used to it, increasing the inhalation and exhalation to 5 or 6 counts. Take your time though.

YOUR POSTURE

To ensure optimum energy flow it's necessary to learn about your posture. Although it's not absolutely essential and the energy will still flow, I've found that I can work more efficiently, more powerfully and for longer, if I have the correct posture. What happens if you have a kink in a straw, or a hosepipe? The flow of water is impeded significantly compared to it being straightened out. It's the same theory.

The following exercises are standing exercises based on Tai chi principles and should not be underestimated. I once collapsed in a Tai Chi class while apparently 'standing still' in this way so only do them for a few minutes to begin with and stop if you feel the need. Exercise 1 can help you to understand any areas of tension within your body. Exercise 2 increases the energy flow and is also useful in centring which I will cover later in this book. Both exercises provide a useful time for relaxation and meditation allowing your energy to circulate at its optimum with as few kinks as possible. Even though it looks like you're just standing around, they are potentially powerful tools for re-energising your whole being.

Practise these exercises in a quiet room, or with calm background music. In good weather you could do them outside to really feel your connection with the universe.

NOTE: If you feel uncomfortable, perhaps as though you're over-heating, discontinue the exercise straight away and ground yourself (see page 38).

Tai Chi Style Exercise 1: **V**
- Stand with your feet shoulder-width apart and parallel, with your toes pointing forward. Drop your chin slightly, looking forward and slightly downwards. Imagine a string attached to your crown (located on the top of your head, slightly towards the back). It pulls your head very slightly up while your body hangs from it like a puppet.
- Curve the upper back slightly and soften the chest area. Your pelvis should be slightly tilted by engaging your abdominal muscles and tucking the base of your spine under. You should feel your spine lengthening as your crown is pulled up and the base of your spine gently curls under.
- Relax the hips and waist and allow your lower body to sink slightly.
- Your shoulders are relaxed with your arms loosely hanging by your side. Allow

your fingers to curve gently in a relaxed way.
- Your knees should be soft. Splay your toes slightly and rock gently back and forth on your feet to find a balance. Think about the point between the pads of your first and second toes, known as 'Bubbling Spring' (more on this later). Once you feel balanced, stand still and imagine roots extending out deep into the ground from this point.
- Breathe normally and stand quietly in this way for five minutes.
- If you feel any tension creeping into your body, consciously relax the area. Take your awareness to the point of tension, take a deep slow breath in and out. If necessary mentally say the word ' relax' slowly three times as you breathe deeply.
- Over time you may wish to build up to 10 minutes as you get used to the positioning.

Tai Chi Style Exercise 2: V
- Start in the position from Exercise 1.
- Bend your knees slightly and sink down. Maintaining a relaxed posture move your arms forward (leading with the forearms) round in front of your body as though you are holding a giant ball between your hands and chest. Your fingers should be relaxed, slightly separated from each other and pointing towards the opposite knee.
- The line of your arms from shoulder to fingertips should create a gentle curve as though following the line of a giant beach ball or balloon. Pay particular attention to your wrists, they shouldn't create an angle as this will impede energy flow into the hands.
- Relax your shoulder blades down your back.
- Remember to think about the invisible thread pulling you up from your crown.
- Breathe normally and stand quietly in this way for five minutes.
- Relax and enjoy the posture being aware of any sensations around your body, like heat or tingling. Again, be aware of and rectify any areas of tension.
- Over time you may wish to build up to 10 minutes as you get used to the positioning.

YOUR HANDS

Being aware of, sensing or feeling spiritual energy is not something that most people are used to. However, we are used to touching and feeling with our hands, so they are a great place to start this process.

There are chakras in the palms of the hands, albeit smaller than the seven main ones down the centre of the body. Almost immediately that you start to work with energy you should become aware of them. There are also even smaller chakras along the fingers that may make their presence felt as you progress and become more experienced, although this doesn't always happen and makes little difference to your abilities. The diagram below shows the smaller chakras as I sense them, including one just at the wrist joint that I have only recently become aware of.

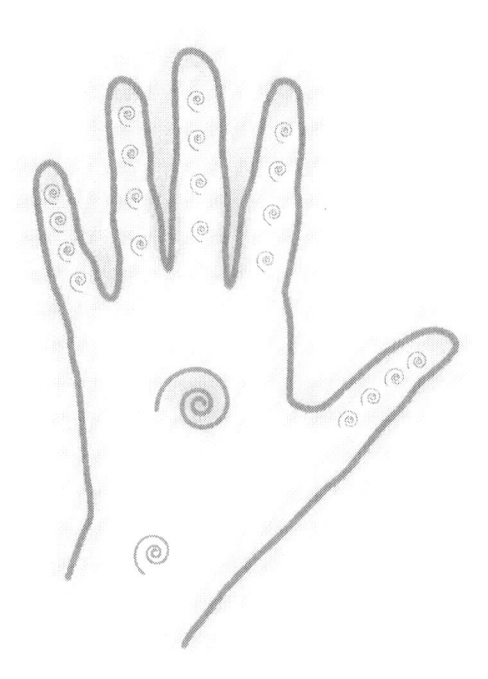

The beauty of energy work is that it's your intention that's of paramount importance. Whether you're aware of the sensations in your own (physical or energetic) body or of the effects that you have on others is irrelevant. Those you work with will feel your impact and benefit from it regardless, and that's what counts. If you find it hard to feel the energy, the feedback that you receive from others should give you the confidence and belief to continue until you do become aware of these things yourself.

Our hands are used in almost every aspect of energy work from giving healing physically, and often remotely, scanning the aura for hotspots, leaks or other problems, directing energy, and for more advanced energy and psychic development practises, such as working with crystals, dowsing and automatic writing.

The hands are great sensors once you begin to use them, ask most healers about this and I'm sure they would confirm it. I know from my own experiences as well as from my Reiki students, that once you're conscious of this area of your energy system you will never be unaware of it again. I can feel energy in my hands whenever it's needed by me, or by someone close by and on numerous other occasions. Suffice to say my hands are my early warning system that let me know that my ability to channel energy is needed. As I write and re-read this, my hands are tingling away like mad!

A Japanese technique that I use regularly is 'Gassho'. This literally means 'to place the two palms together'. Initially it's a sign of reverence and respect and does appear to simply be placing your hands together in prayer position. But with the correct practise and intention it can be very useful in energy work.

Firstly, by using it at the start of any energy work it states your intention to do just that, to step out of everyday mode and begin your work on a higher vibrational level. The Gassho is said to bring opposites together, creating unity in the body by bringing the left and right sides together, also integrating the body and mind as one. It's a great meditation technique. In Japanese culture, a firm Gassho indicates a quiet and focused mind. I've also found that it activates my palm chakras, creates a circuit within my energy system and allows my to build up energy reserves. If you're feeling cold, try using this circuit to generate internal energy to warm your physical body - I find this very useful.

I have described 'Gassho' along with some other practical exercises to help you become aware of and activate the chakras and energy in your hands. They're not simply to be done once but should be practised regularly as part of your development process. They will help you to become aware of energy and also assist you in feeling, understanding, channelling, and using the energy. Take your time and don't expect to 'get it' first time round. You might, but you might not. Practice and perseverance are essential.

Exercise 1 - How to practise Gassho: **V**
- Place your hands together, palm-to-palm in front of your face (one fist distance between the fingers and the tip of the nose).
- Your fingers are straight and the palms are pressed slightly together.
- Your elbows are raised and aren't touching the body and the forearms are almost but not quite parallel with the floor.
- Your eyes must be kept focussed on the tips of the middle fingers.
- Maintain this position for a few minutes, breathing normally.
- Keep your shoulders relaxed and don't allow tension to creep into your body.
- Be aware of any sensations around or within your body.

When I use Gassho to begin any energy work I like to hold the position as described here, to make my connection and then I bring my hands, still palm to palm, down to my heart chakra for a short while before continuing with my work.

Exercise 2 - Feel the Energy **V**
- Sit comfortably in a chair with your feet flat on the floor.
- Place your palms together and focus your attention on their contact with each other. You may become aware of heat building up.
- After a minute or so separate your hands very slightly. Maintain your focus on the space between your palms. Very slowly move your hands slightly away from and then towards each other, as though pumping the air between the palms. You should become aware of some resistance here.
- Very gradually take your hands further apart and as they come back towards each other, still with that pumping action, make the gap between your palms larger and larger. Feel as though there is a ball of energy between your palms. This energy has been created through the smaller chakras in the palms of your hands using your auric energy.
- You can play with the energy with practice. Move your hands around and imagine you are holding a small ball, feel the edges of it and imagine that there

is energy or light coming from your palms filling this ball up. You may feel it expand, requiring your hands to move further apart. This is a safe exercise to play with and assists you in beginning to feel the energy that we talk of and activating the chakras in your hands.

Exercise 3 - Feel the Aura <u>V</u>
- If you can, work with a friend for this exercise, although you can also use plants, children and animals, if they'll stay still long enough (I certainly hope the plants do, otherwise you have a real problem!)
- Ask your friend to stand and close their eyes.
- From a few feet away, slowly walk towards the subject with your hands outstretched. If you feel that you wish to pause then do so. This is probably the edge of an auric layer, most likely the emotional aura. At this point, slowly move your hands around the outline of the subject at the same distance from their physical body. You may feel hot or cold spots, these can indicate energy blockages and can sometimes relate to physical problems as well.
- Discuss any imbalance that you have picked up on with your friend and get their feedback too. You may find that a 'hotspot' in a particular area makes perfect sense to them for example, heat around a joint or muscle area may be as a result of a previous sports injury or joint problem.

Exercise 4 - The Hand Game <u>V</u>
- You will need to work with a friend for this exercise. Stand or sit opposite each other and place your hands in front of you, so that your palms are facing those of your friend, about one inch away from them. One person should close their eyes.
- The other keeps their eyes open and moves their hands slowly and deliberately around in the space between you.
- The partner whose eyes are closed should attempt to sense any movement and move their hands to match their partner's – without physical contact.
- Swap over and try it the other way around.
- You could try this with an observer and ask that the active partner simply move their hands into 10 positions within the space between you. The observer could record the number of 'hits' where the 'sensor' correctly moves their hands to mirror the others. As you get better, you should see an improvement in these scores.

○ You may find that you work better with a certain person than you do with others. This may be because you have a different rapport, a closer bond, or perhaps a more physical relationship so are used to each other's energy on a subconscious level.

YOUR FEET

As with the palms of the hands, the soles of the feet have chakras. I believe there is a major one in the centre of the sole and smaller ones in various other positions including along the toes. You may be wondering why they're important, "Surely we're not going to give healing with our feet?" I can hear you ask. Well no, not normally anyway. I am able to feel energy emitting from my feet and I've known this to be very useful on occasion. It means I can give healing to cats and dogs who are happy to curl up by my feet but might not accept being held. Also if someone were to have a physical disability that would make using their hands difficult or impossible, there is no reason, cleanliness allowing, that they couldn't use their feet.

However, my main reason for talking about the feet is in understanding a number of points and techniques essential to any form of energy work.

The feet chakras allow us to 'plug into' the universal energy system, meaning that we can generate, very often, massive amounts of energy and work at a high level for extended periods of time. We can also use them to ground our energy. When used with the other techniques in this book they help us to remain focussed and to channel and utilise universal energy in an accomplished way very quickly. Here we will focus on grounding as it's such an important technique but the other elements will also be covered later in this book.

'Bubbling Spring'
This is an important point on the foot to be aware of. Also known as 'kidney 1' in acupuncture and shiatsu, or the 'solar plexus reflex point' in reflexology, it's below the ball of the foot in the depression between the first and second toe. It's most easily found if you run your thumb from the inside edge of the ball of the foot, following its line round and up.

'Bubbling Spring' is a very important point as it's said to be the entry point into our personal energetic system for earth energy. It's from here that I always visualise my main connection with the earth and I find this very powerful. 'Bubbling Spring' is vital in Tai Chi and Chi Kung practise. By being aware of it and grounding yourself through this point you will, apart from anything else, find that you have better balance physically as well as energetically.

As mentioned previously, there is also a main chakra in the centre of the soles of the feet, level with the arch. It can take up a lot of the sole when it's more developed. Both this chakra and 'Bubbling Spring' can be used for energy work. I have found that generally I use 'Bubbling Spring' for grounding and to pull earth energy in, and that the sole chakra is best used for energy to flow out. However, if I wish, I can use both points simultaneously to draw in energy for high level or prolonged energy work. I guess which works best and for what purpose is a matter for debate, but what is important is that you use a method that works for you. I'm giving you information on both methods so that you can practise the exercises here and decide which way you prefer to work.

The diagram below shows 'Bubbling Spring' and the sole chakra along with smaller chakras, where I sense them to be, including one at the centre of the heel that I have only recently become aware of.

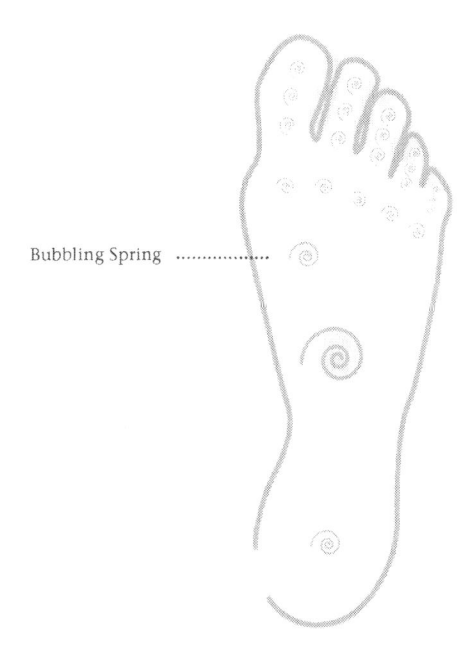

Bubbling Spring

Grounding

Grounding should be done at the end of every session of meditation, energetic or psychic work. It brings us back to earth and reconnects us with the physical world, after time spent connecting with the spiritual realms, allowing us to concentrate again on more worldly matters. When we do energy work our vibratory rate increases and our awareness expands to put us in touch with and to encompass the higher energy levels with which we need to work. Grounding lowers our energy vibrations back to a more physical level so that we can function again in this dimension.

If you don't ground your energies sufficiently you may feel spaced out for a while after working or meditating. You will also be extremely sensitive and pick up on all sorts of energies and emotions from others and from your surroundings. Grounding can be done at any time when you feel a bit 'away with the fairies' or 'spaced out' and can be done in combination with protective techniques whenever it's felt necessary. As much as we would often like to, we can't continue to be as connected on a higher spiritual or energetic level in daily life, it's just not practical. The following grounding exercises utilise the feet as they're the lowest point of our energetic and physical body and most easily in contact with the earth energies that assist in our grounding. If the exercise is insufficient and you still feel a bit spaced out, you can try walking around for a little while. Stamping your feet or jumping up and down also help to bring you back to the physical world. Another method is to find and hold on to any crystals that are associated with grounding as they help to pull your energy back to a more physical resonance. The best are Black Tourmaline, Black Obsidian, Apache Tear and Black Kyanite. Just hold them, or pop them in your pocket. These can also be useful on a daily basis if you have a tendency to 'drift off' or be a daydreamer. If these methods don't do the trick, you can ground your energy very readily by eating a small amount of food such as a biscuit. This brings your physical body back into the equation and disconnects you from the spiritual work. After working with a group we frequently find ourselves having late night chocolate or tea and toast - just don't over eat as this can cause nausea after energy work.

Closing and Grounding Visualisation 1- for use after specific work & meditations when you have consciously 'opened' your energy field. <u>A</u>
NOTE: If you work better sitting on the floor you can ground yourself by visualising the energy going out into the earth through the base of the spine rather than the soles of the feet.

- Sit in a comfortable position and close your eyes.
- Bring your attention to your breathing and focus on this for a few breaths.
- Take your awareness to the invisible energy field surrounding your physical body. If you can't sense it, simply imagine it as a bubble a few inches around you.
- Visualise it drawing in and closing around your physical body like plastic shrink-wrap.
- Take your awareness to the area just above your crown and see a sphere of light sitting here.
- Imagine that sphere of light shrinking in size until it's tiny and then sinking down through the crown of your head.
- See it slowly descending down past the brow into the throat.
- Then following the line of the spine, down, through your body, towards your heart area.
- Down to your solar plexus, through the abdominal area, to the base of your spine.
- Now visualise the sphere of energy either leaving through the base of your spine, or dividing in two and sinking down through your legs and leaving through the soles of your feet.
- Feel this energy leaving you and connecting with the earth.
- Have a sense of downward movement, deep into the earth.
- Become more aware of your feet and your physical body.
- Take a moment to thank your spirit guides, angels and loved ones in spirit for their presence, protection and wisdom whilst you've been working. Knowing that they will always be on hand should you need to call on them.
- Now bring your awareness back to your physical body, the chair you are sitting on, your contact with the floor.
- Begin to bring some movement back into your fingers and toes.
- In your own time, open your eyes, fully awake and aware and in the physical world.

Grounding Visualisation 2 – for other times or just when you feel a bit spacey.
- Sit in a comfortable position and close your eyes.
- Bring your attention to your breathing and focus on this for a few breaths.
- Imagine that you have thick roots, like the roots of an oak tree, growing from the soles of your feet.
- Visualise these roots going through the floor, down into the earth and down

further into the centre of the earth, anchoring you and keeping you grounded.

- Once you've visualised these roots anchoring you to the ground, bring your awareness back, slowly and gently to your physical body.
- In your own time, open your eyes, fully awake and aware and in the physical world.

YOUR CENTRE

We all know that occasional feeling of being completely content, happy and peaceful. I certainly hope you've experienced it at least once. Being centred on an energetic level helps us to foster this feeling whenever we wish. And with regular practice it can help us to carry this feeling into everyday life. Feeling centred helps us to cope, to understand, to remain balanced and to act in an unprejudiced manner. In my opinion, regular meditation and energy work on ourselves will encourage a sense of being centred, but there's also some specific energy work you can do to actively centre your own energy.

Sacral Centre or 'Hara'
The word 'hara' literally means stomach, abdomen or belly. Energy is said to be stored here and to expand from this point throughout the entire physical and subtle body.

Connecting with our energy through the hara is said to ensure good health and provide access to a reliable source of strength whenever needed. In Tai Chi and Chi Kung, this area is known as the 'Tan Tien' It is this area that we use to centre our energy.

Use the centring exercise here to help increase your energy reserves, to find peace and calm within yourself, or prior to meditation. Sometimes centring is referred to in exercises and workbooks too, so now you'll know one way to do it.

Centring Your Energy: A
- Sitting comfortably, bring your attention to the centre of your being, the lower abdominal area. Gently place your hands here.
- Focus on your breathing; become aware of the rise and fall of your abdomen. As you inhale it will gently rise and as you exhale it will fall.
- Feel a sense of warmth here.
- In your mind's eye allow a symbol or shape to form. It may be a simple glow of light, a flame or a flower. Imagine that this symbol or shape is sitting at, and represents, your centre.
- With each in-breath visualise your symbol becoming larger, stronger or more open, whichever is appropriate.
- With each out-breath, imagine that you are exhaling any negativity left from your day, physical discomforts, or worries that you may have.
- Continue with this exercise for a few minutes. However, if you feel uncomfortable or begin to overheat then stop.
- When you wish to finish this exercise simply remove your hands from your centre and take your attention to your next activity. If you are finishing your work here then focus on grounding your energy (see page 38).

YOUR CROWN

The crown chakra is located on the top of the head, slightly towards the back. (Think about the positioning of a Jewish man's cap). It energetically connects us to the spiritual plane and becomes more open with spiritual advancement. In Tai Chi, this is where it's considered that all the meridian lines converge and that from here excess energy is released up into the atmosphere.

We are always connected to the divine source and channelling universal energy by the very fact that we're alive. However, we have so much else that we have to think about and focus on, whether it's eating, working or exercising, that we don't always acknowledge this connection, let alone consciously work with it.

We can use visualisations of the crown chakra to work with the universal energy around us and to integrate it within us for positive change, spiritual and psychic development and for helping others. It's another essential element of learning to work with energy.

To begin to feel the energy at the crown can take time, so I've included some simple exercises to get you started. Work through them in order, one after the other so that the energy has a chance to build up. As it does so, it should become easier for you to feel, although you may need to repeat them a number of times before you start to feel it fully. However, even if you can't always feel it, simply believe it and visualise it and it will work for you. Ensure that you use the grounding exercise on page 38 when you're finished.

Crown Exercise 1: <u>V</u>
- Sit comfortably and relax your body.
- Breathe slowly and deeply.
- Place the palm of one hand on the crown of your head and breathe deeply for a slow count of 20.
- Remove your hand but maintain your awareness of the crown. It should be warm where your hand has been. Keep your attention there for another count of 20 imagining that your hand is still placed there.
- The feeling of warmth and slight pressure should remain on your crown throughout.

Crown Exercise 2: <u>V</u>
- Practise Gassho:
- Place your hands together, palm-to-palm in front of your face (one fist distance between the fingers and the tip of the nose). Your fingers are straight and the palms are pressed slightly together. Your elbows are not touching the body and the forearms are almost but not quite parallel with the floor. Your eyes must be kept on the tips of the middle fingers. Hold this position for a count of 20 whilst breathing slowly and deeply. You should become aware of warmth growing in the palms of the hands.
- Place the palm of one hand on the crown of your head and breathe deeply for a slow count of 20. You can place the other hand in your lap.
- Remove your hand and return to Gassho but maintain your awareness of the crown. It should be warm where your hand has been. Keep your attention here for another count of 20.
- The feeling of warmth and slight pressure should remain on your crown throughout.

Crown Exercise 3:
- Practise Gassho:
- Place your hands together, palm-to-palm in front of the face (one fist distance between the fingers and the tip of the nose). The fingers are straight and the palms are pressed slightly together. The elbows are not touching the body and the forearms are almost but not quite parallel with the floor. The eyes must be kept on the tips of the middle fingers. Hold this position for a count of 20 whilst breathing slowly and deeply. You should become aware of warmth growing in the palms of the hands.
- Maintain Gassho but take your awareness to your crown recalling the feeling that you had after you had placed your hand here previously. Keep your attention here, recalling the feeling of warmth and slight pressure for another count of 20.

Crown Chakra Visualisation:
- Sit comfortably and relax your body.
- Breathe slowly and deeply.
- Take your awareness to your crown.
- Imagine a beam of pure white light coming down from above and touching the crown of your head. Maintain this visualisation for a few minutes making a mental note of any sensations that you may feel in or around your body, or any images that pop into your mind.

As you become practised at working with the crown chakra you'll find it easier and easier to feel the energy here. This is just the start, we'll do more work with the crown chakra when we practise opening our energy field.

BRINGING IT ALL TOGETHER

Once you have an understanding of, and some practical experience with all of the component parts that we've looked at so far, it's much easier to bring it all together. You've probably had a sense of the energy already through the previous exercises but when it all comes together it's really powerful.

Here's the process to follow to bring it all together: Before undertaking energy or light work, healing, readings, or working with spirit you need to put energetic protection in place, ensure you're relaxed, then establish a 'conscious connection' with the universal energy source, then open your energy field and awareness to allow you to work at a higher vibrational level. Once you have completed your energy, spiritual or psychic work your should ensure that you close and ground your energy. Here I have listed the process from the start. It includes some of the exercises you have already done and then takes you in to the new ones.

Energetic Protection
I have already covered the theory of this on page 20. Use this protection request before starting your energy work.

- Take a moment to close your eyes and calm your mind.
- Concentrate on your breathing, allowing the breath to become deeper and slower.
- Mentally ask your spirit guides and angels to draw close and offer their assistance using the following script:

"I call upon my spirit guides, angels and loved ones in spirit to draw close to me and to create a circle of protection around me ensuring that I am safe and protected at all times and on all levels while I work and afterwards. I ask for your protection, guidance and wisdom.
(If working with spiritual / psychic development add in the following:
I am happy to work with guidance from the spirit world and to communicate with them, but I do so only in love and light and with the highest intentions. I ask that anyone from the spirit world who wishes to assist or communicate does so with the same intentions, and that my spirit guides and angels enforce this on my behalf.)"

Relaxation A

- Sit or lie comfortably.
- Take your awareness to your hands, make a tight fist, hold for a count of three and release.
- Tense your lower arms, hold for three, and release.
- Tense your upper arms, hold for three, and release.
- Tense your shoulders, lifting them up towards your ears, hold for three, and release.
- Take your awareness to your neck: pull your chin down towards your chest but

keep it from touching chest, hold for three and then release.
- Take your awareness to your lower face and jaw, bite hard and pull back the corners of your mouth hold for three and then release.
- Now, open your mouth wide as though you are yawning, hold for 3, then release.
- Screw your eyes up and wrinkle your nose, hold for three and then release.
- Move your awareness to your forehead, lift your eyebrows as high as possible, hold for three and then release.
- Take your awareness to your upper torso, pull your shoulder blades together hold for three and then release.
- Tense your stomach muscles, pulling your bellybutton in towards your spine, hold for three and then release.
- Taking your awareness to your legs tense your thigh muscles, hold for three and then release.
- Pull your toes towards your head tensing your calf muscles hold for three and then release.
- Taking your awareness to your feet, point and curl toes downwards, hold for three and then release.
- Tense your whole body at once, hands, arms, face, neck, chest, stomach, thighs, calves and feet, screw your eyes up, hold for three, two, one, and completely release.
- *(Move straight on to the next stage.)*

Breathing A
- Take your awareness to your breathing, preferably through your nose, as this is more relaxing.
- Ensure that you are breathing slowly and deeply.
- As you inhale, your abdomen will gently rise. And as you exhale it will fall.
- If your mind drifts or you lose track during this exercise bring your attention back to refocus on your breathing.
- Take a long, slow, deep inhalation for a count of 1 - 2 - 3 - 4, hold for 1- 2 and exhale for 1 - 2 - 3 - 4.
- In 2 3 4, Hold *(pause)*, Out 2 3 4
- In 2 3 4, Hold *(pause)*, Out 2 3 4
- In 2 3 4, Hold *(pause)*, Out 2 3 4
- In 2 3 4, Hold *(pause)*, Out 2 3 4

- In 2 3 4, Hold *(pause)*, Out 2 3 4
- Continue breathing slowly and deeply until you're ready to move on to the next stage. It's not a race or a competition, just a way of relaxing and focusing your mind on the moment.
- You can start to lengthen the breath once you're used to it, increasing the inhalation and exhalation to 5 or 6 counts. Take your time though.
- Continue in this way, focusing on the breath and counting. If your mind drifts or you lose track, start counting again and refocus on your breathing. It's not a race or a competition, just a way of relaxing and focusing your mind on the moment.
- You can start to lengthen the breath once you're used to it, increasing the inhalation and exhalation to 5 or 6 counts. Take your time though.
- Allow yourself 5 – 10 minutes to fully relax.

Centring A

- Sitting comfortably, bring your attention to the centre of your being, the lower abdominal area. Gently place your hands here.
- Focus on your breathing; become aware of the rise and fall of your abdomen. As you inhale it will gently rise and as you exhale it will fall.
- Feel a sense of warmth here.
- In your mind's eye allow a symbol or shape to form. It may be a simple glow of light, a flame or a flower. Imagine that this symbol or shape is sitting at, and represents, your centre.
- With each in-breath visualise your symbol becoming larger, stronger or more open, whichever is appropriate.
- With each out-breath, imagine that you are exhaling any negativity left from your day, physical discomforts, or worries that you may have.
- Continue with this exercise for a few minutes. However, if you feel uncomfortable or begin to overheat then stop.
- When you wish to finish this exercise simply remove your hands from your centre and take your attention to your next activity. If you are finishing your work here then focus on grounding your energy (see page 38).

Conscious Connection

For me, this is just like putting a battery into an item to complete a circuit and create power. This universal energy circuit is always around us and we're always a part of it. Conscious connection allows us to step outside of our everyday reality and fully integrate with it once more. Sometimes people are taught only to connect to the higher realms through the crown chakra and then at the end of their work, to ground through their feet, and this does work. However, I've found that by starting with and maintaining a conscious connection at both the feet and crown throughout, I can create a more controlled and focussed energy flow. It also allows a much larger amount of energy to be channelled. If during your work you start to lose focus, feel less energy flowing or need an extra boost, then re-establishing your conscious connection will remedy this. It's a very simple exercise but don't under estimate the difference it will make to your work and abilities. The following visualisation should be done after putting protective measures in place. Try it and sit or stand allowing your energy to flow, observing any sensations. Also try it in combination with the Tai Chi style standing exercises on pages 30-31. I prefer to do this when standing for a more powerful effect.

Conscious Connection Visualisation: - A

- You can sit comfortably either cross-legged on the floor or upright in a chair or you can stand.
- Take your awareness to the soles of your feet, feeling their contact with the floor.
- Visualise lines of energy extending out from your feet (either from the chakra point, or bubbling spring) and down into the ground. In your mind's eye, see these lines of energy as roots extending deep into the earth. Maintain this feeling of energy at the feet and be aware of the earth energy as it travels back up through these roots entering your energy system, revitalising and nourishing you. It may help to see them beginning to glow with light as the energy moves through them up from the earth entering your energy system, making you feel deeply connected and very strong and powerful.
- Now take your awareness to the crown of your head. Imagine that you are being suspended by a piece of string from this point. The piece of string hangs from a point far above you, so far above you that you are unable to see its origin. You should have a sense of being lifted upwards.
- In your mind's eye, the string is a brilliant white light, a magical connection

with higher realms. Its brilliance and its power connects with and enters into your energy system, making you feel amazingly empowered.

Opening
'Opening' is a term that we use to describe the process by which we alter and expand our energies and our awareness, so that we can work on a more spiritual level. We take our awareness beyond our physical bodies so that we are able to tap into the unseen energies that exist at a higher vibration. This is where we need to be when we're working with spiritual and psychic development exercises. We can use our understanding of auras and chakras to help 'open' our awareness. Primarily this is done through visualisation, until we are able to sense or feel the energy changes that are described. Opening consists of two elements, elevating and expansion of your energies.

Part 1 - Elevating Your Energy: <u>A</u>
- Take your awareness back to your feet and to the energy entering through your soles; imagine it travelling up through your legs to the base of your spine.
- At the base of the spine imagine that the energy becomes a sphere of deep red mist or light. As you visualise it, it becomes more vibrant in colour.
- From this point a beam of energy leaves the red sphere and travels up towards the sacral area, just below the belly button. Here it forms a sphere of vibrant orange mist or light. As you focus on it, it becomes stronger in colour.
- Gradually, a beam of energy leaves the orange sphere and travels up towards the solar plexus, where it forms a sphere of clear yellow. With each breath, this yellow becomes stronger and brighter.
- Once more a beam of energy leaves this sphere and continues its journey up to the heart area. Here a sphere of mist or light begins to form, which you may see as either green or pink. Focus on this area for a few breaths allowing the energy to grow stronger and clearer and it may begin to expand.
- Gradually, a beam of energy leaves the heart area and moves upwards to the throat. Here it forms a sphere of clear blue. Once more, as you focus on this area, allow the colour to expand and increase in strength.
- Now, visualise a strand of energy leaving the throat area and linking with the third eye area, just between and slightly above the eyes. Here energy will begin to form as before. You may see this energy as either a rich indigo or violet,

whichever you prefer. Concentrate on this energy and visualise it increasing in strength and energy.
- This beam of light extends upwards moving up to the crown. As it does so, become aware of a beam of energy coming down from high above to meet the first at the crown. A sphere of pure energy begins to form in this area. You may see this energy as either violet or pure white light. This connects you with the higher realms of spirit.

Part 2 - Expanding Your Awareness: A
- As you hold this vision for a few breaths the light grows and strengthens. The sphere becomes larger and brighter and as it does so, the beautiful pure light begins to overflow down and around you, surrounding you in this wonderful energy.
- It fills your aura, cleansing, balancing and strengthening it.
- The light around your physical body grows stronger and brighter. It extends out in all directions around you. See in your mind's eye how far it extends.
- Now take a deep slow breath in and as you slowly exhale, imagine your aura expanding further as though you're blowing it up like a balloon but maintaining its strength and brightness.
- Continue to breathe in this way, expanding your energy further with each out breath. As you do so, you feel safe and comfortable. You feel relaxed and light.

Closing and Grounding
As described on page 38, closing and grounding should be done at the end of every session of meditation or psychic work. As with 'opening', visualisation is the main method that we use for closing and grounding our energies. Here's a visualisation to use.
NOTE: If you work better sitting on the floor you can ground yourself by visualising the energy going out into the earth through the base of the spine rather than the soles of the feet.

Closing and Grounding Visualisation - for use after specific work & meditations when you have consciously 'opened' your energy field.
- Sit in a comfortable position and close your eyes.
- Bring your attention to your breathing and focus on it for a few breaths.

- Take your awareness to the invisible energy field that you expanded around you previously. Visualise it drawing in and closing around your physical body.
- Take your awareness to the area just above your crown and see a sphere of light sitting here.
- Imagine that sphere of light shrinking in size until it's tiny before it sinks down through the crown of your head.
- See it slowly descending down past the brow into the throat.
- Then following the line of the spine, down, through your body, towards your heart area.
- Down to your solar plexus, through the abdominal area, to the base of your spine.
- Now visualise the sphere of energy either leaving through the base of your spine, or dividing in two and sinking down through your legs and leaving through the soles of your feet.
- Feel this energy leaving you and connecting with the earth.
- Have a sense of downward movement, deep into the earth.
- Become more aware of your feet and your physical body.
- Take a moment to thank your spirit guides, angels and loved ones in spirit for their presence, protection and wisdom whilst you have been working. Knowing that they will always be on hand should you need to call on them.
- Now bring your awareness back to your physical body, the chair you are sitting on, your contact with the floor.
- Begin to bring some movement back in to your fingers and toes.
- In your own time, open your eyes, fully awake and aware and in the physical world.

- If you don't feel completely back in the room walk around for a little while. Stamping your feet or jumping up and down helps to bring you back to the physical world. If these don't do the trick remember that you can ground your energy very readily by eating a small amount of food such as a biscuit.

POWER POINTS

- In summary, when undertaking energy work, the following checklist should be followed to ensure that you are working at your optimum and to ensure that you don't suffer any negative effects during or after working.

    - Protection
    - Relaxation
    - Connection
    - Opening – Elevation & Expansion
    - Your chosen energy work (meditation, healing etc.)
    - Closing and Grounding

- Centring can be done at any time for focus or to reconnect with or increase your energy flow.
- Go back and practise the exercises in this chapter repeatedly. Try to set aside some time each day to work through them in turn and see how your experiences change.
- Try classes in yoga, Tai Chi, or Chi Kung which will all help you to understand your energy flow better.
- You could have regular healing or join a healing circle to help to develop your skills and sensitivity. Plus you will get feedback from others which will help you even more in your progress.

USE THE POWER

"The more willing you are to surrender to the energy within you, the more power can flow through you."

Shakti Gawain
(Author & personal development teacher)

In this section we will go through a number of exercises and ideas of how you can connect with and use universal energy. If you don't feel that you're ready, continue working with the previous exercises until you wish to progress. Bear in mind though that the only way to really learn about the energy is to start to use it. Persevere and where possible, work with others to get feedback.

WORKING WITH YOUR ENERGY FIELD

Using energy exercises, breathing, and visualisation can have a positive impact on our own energies. The exercises provided here will give you a good grounding in working with your aura and provide essential techniques for use in further energy work. Where there are two exercises with the same intention, try them both at different times and see which one works best for you.

Remember, to get the most out of your energy work, you should follow the procedure mentioned previously before each session:
- Protection
- Relaxation
- Connection
- Opening – Elevation and Expansion

- Your chosen energy work
- And end with the closing and grounding exercise.

Having said that, the following four exercises can be easily and safely performed whenever they are needed, so if you have been in a room, building or situation that has made you feel uncomfortable or felt strange in some way you may want to do a cleansing visualisation when you leave. If you feel a bit low on energy you may need to use the energy boost, or if you feel awkward in a social situation, or that someone is being a little negative towards you, simply use the 'zipping up' exercise. At first you may need to take yourself off somewhere to do these exercises alone (even if it's just locking yourself in a toilet cubicle!). But in time, you will be able to quietly visualise what you need to do and you'll feel and know that it's worked just as well.

Cleansing Your Aura

Cleanse Your Aura: Exercise 1 <u>A</u>
- Sitting comfortably, bring your attention to the centre of your being, the lower abdominal area. Gently place your hands there.
- You may want to close your eyes.
- Focus on your breathing; become aware of the rise and fall of your abdomen. As you inhale it will gently rise and as you exhale it will fall. Feel a sense of warmth here as you take a few slow deep breaths.
- Link your hands gently on your lap and imagine that you're holding a white candle in your hands at your centre.
- See the candle alight.
- Breathe slowly and deeply.
- As you breathe, visualise the candle flame increasing in strength. It does not get any bigger, but the light that it gives off, a pure white light, does. It grows with each breath eventually filling your entire aura with a brilliant glow. As it does so, it encompasses and purifies any negativity, any stress and any impurities or energies that you may have picked up from others.
- Visualise your auric energy being filled with this pure white light, any damage is healed, your aura becomes perfectly shaped, symmetrically oval, extending out in all directions around you, above and below you.

- Continue with this visualisation for a few minutes, mentally checking your aura for anything that isn't perfect. However, if you feel uncomfortable or begin to overheat then stop.
- When you wish to finish this exercise simply remove your hands from your centre and take your attention to your next activity. If you're finishing your work here then ground your energy.

Cleanse Your Aura: Exercise 2 <u>A</u>
- Sit comfortably and close your eyes.
- Imagine that there's a small whirlwind just above you in the air. See it in your mind's eye as silver and white. See it spinning, gaining momentum and then lowering down until the base of the whirlwind enters your crown chakra.
- As it does so, it gets larger, spinning through and down the central axis of your body and extending out through your entire aura.
- As it spins, it sends any negativity flying away from you to be dissipated into the earth.
- When you feel that your aura is cleansed and refreshed, visualise the whirlwind shrinking in size and sinking down through your feet and into the earth grounding any negativity that will be recycled by earthly energy.
- You should feel refreshed and invigorated.
- Take your attention to your next activity, or if you're finishing your work here then ground your energy.

Boost Your Energy Levels: <u>A</u>
- Practise Gassho as follows:
- Place your hands together, palm-to-palm in front of your face (one fist distance between the fingers and the tip of the nose).
- Your fingers are straight and the palms are pressed slightly together.
- Your elbows are not touching the body and the forearms are almost but not quite parallel with the floor.
- Your eyes must be kept on the tips of the middle fingers.
- Maintain this position while breathing slowly and deeply.
- You may wish to close your eyes as you take your awareness to your crown and visualise a brilliant white light flowing in through the crown chakra. As you do so, mentally ask for it to be energised and imagine it changing slightly so that

it now contains gold light too.
- Imagine this gold and white light pouring in through the crown, passing down the centre line of your body to your heart chakra. Here, visualise it splitting in two and moving along your arms to your hands.
- Take your awareness to the palms of your hands and to the slight gap created here.
- Feel the energy passing through from one hand to another and connecting together. As it does this it creates a circuit that will move around in a clockwise manner, through your arms, gaining momentum as it does, creating a golden flow of energy all around you. The energy flows around your arms faster and faster.
- See the circle that it creates growing so that it exists outside of your arms as well now, getting wider and wider, filling your aura.
- As the energy continues to flow the golden circle expands upwards and downwards creating a tube of golden light spinning and swirling all around you.
- Let the energy flow for as long as you feel comfortable with it and then thank the energy for giving you a boost. Imagine the tube sliding upwards and away back towards the heavens leaving you feeling full of energy and in a wonderfully positive state of mind.
- Take your attention to your next activity or if you are finishing your work here then ground your energy.

Zipping Up

I learnt this exercise from a friend studying Health Kinesiology and having tried it a number of times felt that I had to add it to this book. It's an exercise that utilises the energy of the central line of our energetic system. There appears to be a few variations on this exercise, but all with the same fundamentals and intention. We call it 'zipping up' and many online resources refer to Donna Eden's book 'Energy Medicine' as the initial source of this exercise.
The theory is that if you would like to maintain your energy, prevent others taking it, or you accidentally taking theirs, if you're feeling exposed, out of control or energetically flustered then this exercise will help you. It strengthens the energy of the central meridian and increases it's natural positive flow. It will help you to feel more confident, positive and centred and to think more clearly. It also seems to be a good technique to add to other protective measures, although personally I wouldn't use it in isolation for psychic or energetic protection.

Zipping Up Your Energy: <u>V</u>
- Place one palm at the base of the centre line of your body – on the pubic bone.
- As you inhale slowly move your hand up the midline to your lower lip.
- Perform this routine three times ensuring that each time you return you hand to the base you move it away from your body in a kind of arch. This is so that you don't simply unzip yourself again.

Variations:
Try them all. You never know which method will work for you.
- Some sources suggest that before you do this exercise you should rub your palms together in a circular motion. This will encourage the energy flow at your hands and it's said that this energy will act almost as a magnet so that when you move your hand, your central line energy will automatically be drawn upwards with the movement.
- You may prefer to use 'Gassho' to begin
- Try doing the exercise as described but on your first run through it's slightly different. The first time you do it you're removing any unwanted negative energies. The second and third time you're strengthening your own central line energy as before. Remember to move your hand out away from the body as you return it to the bottom of your 'zip'.
  - Begin with your palm against your body, but then before you begin to move it, turn the palm up and make a slight cup shape with your hand.
  - Run your hand up along the midline as though you're scooping up or gathering any unwanted energy from the central line in the palm of your hand as you go.
  - As you reach your lower lip flip your hand away and out to your side so that you remove the unwanted stuff.
  - Repeat the exercise twice more but with your palm towards your body as before.
- You could even try doing this exercise with your hand as though you're actually holding a zip on a jacket and doing it up to your lip. (Although I would get used the initial method first so that you'll know if this version doesn't work or doesn't feel right for you) I think this is a great way to teach children how to strengthen and protect their energy, especially if they're sensitive souls.
- Once you know what it feels like to 'zip up' you could try simply visualising a

zip up the front of your body doing itself up. This will mean that you can do this exercise absolutely anywhere and no-one will know. It will probably take practice for this to be an effective method for you, especially if you aren't great at visualisation, but if you're used to how it feels using the first method, again, you will know whether this works for you. If the sensation is weaker when using just the visualisation, or you find that you don't feel much of a difference, return to the original physical exercise.

SENSING ENERGY

Interacting With Others' Energies:
When we meet other people or go into places or situations, our auras are the first part of us that pick up on information in the form of energy. This is then filtered down to our conscious mind for interpretation and / or action. For example, if you walk into a room and your aura hits an energy that it doesn't feel comfortable with, it very quickly lets your conscious mind know through a physical sensation or intuitive reaction so that you can choose whether to leave, avoid a particular person or perhaps put energetic protection in place to preserve your energies.

The exercises here will demonstrate how we can affect others and be affected by those around us. It will show the importance of strengthening and protecting your energy field which can be done through a healthy lifestyle, positive thoughts and good visualisation practices.

Exercise 1: How you can affect your aura and others <u>V</u>
- Work with a friend for this exercise.
- One of you (the subject) should stand up or sit in a chair and focus on your own energy field. Visualise it surrounding you.
- When you feel that you're ready visualise or feel it changing shape in some way. You can pull it in close to you, or push it out so that it gets bigger and bigger or push it high above your head. You could also visualise it as a specific colour, as very bright or even moving around you in a particular direction. Once you've chosen what you are going to do, without telling your partner, focus on it completely until your partner notices the change.
- The second person can either sit opposite or walk around, or simply stand next to the subject. It's your role to pick up on any changes or fluctuations in the

subject's aura. You can feel it with your hands, sense the changes or, if you're lucky, you may even see them. Sometimes you will 'see' in your mind's eye and sometimes you will just 'know' what has changed.
- Tell your partner when you pick up on the change and see if you're correct.
- Try two or three different things before swapping over and repeating the exercise.

Exercise 2: How others can affect your aura and you V
- There are a number of ways that you can do this exercise. You can work with one friend or a group.
- One person (the subject) should stand up and close their eyes. Be aware of any sensations that you pick up on around you. You may find that you sway or feel as though you're going to fall in a particular direction. Keeping your eyes shut, tell your partner about the sensations that you are experiencing.
- The other person should stand in front, behind or to one side of the subject. From about two feet away you should use your hands to either push or pull the subject's aura in a specific direction. Work gently and slowly as the subject can be affected quite tangibly by this exercise.
- When the subject says or shows that they can feel the change, swap over and repeat the exercise.
- If you are working in a group larger than two, you can all stand in a circle around the subject at about four feet away. Then one of you should step in slowly and quietly, standing nearer to them until the subject picks up on the energy change and says out loud where the person is or points to them. Take it in turns to be the subject and experience how others can affect your energy in this way.

Scanning
Scanning can be used to pick up fluctuations in the energies surrounding places, objects and people. Scanning works in two ways, firstly because we encourage the natural sensitivity in our palm chakras. Secondly the energy that we channel through our hands kind of 'bounces back' from the energy of the person or object, giving us a form of energetic feedback that we can feel and learn to interpret. Here we will focus on auras to help you get used to the method.

By feeling or 'scanning' someone's aura it's possible to find hot or cold spots, which can indicate an energetic imbalance or area of ill health within the physical body. Scanning is simple but may take practise, the more you do it, the more finely tuned your hands become to different sensations. It's a good idea to start a healing session by 'scanning' the person's aura for areas that may need more healing than others. Some people are able to see the colours of the aura naturally which makes this process quick and easy.

Scanning Exercise V
- Working with a friend, make sure that they are sitting or lying comfortably.
- Practise 'Gassho".
- Consciously connect with universal energy and allow it to begin to flow through you. You may be able to feel it at your palms.
- Start from either the head or the feet and place your hands a few inches above their body.
- Move your hands slowly through their aura until you have covered the entire area of their body.
- You may feel heat, tingling, pulsing or cold areas or you may intuitively know at a certain point that there's an imbalance.
- Discuss your experiences and provide feedback to each other.

NOTE: You cannot use scanning to diagnose a medical condition, it's by no means a scientifically proven method and it's also against the law to do so. However it can be used to understand where a person may need more healing energy, and this very often turns out to be a point where there is a physical problem. Please never scare your friends by telling them that they have a problem. However, if you find an energy imbalance, do discuss it, perhaps you could say 'I am picking up a hotspot around your elbow, which would indicate an energy imbalance, can you think of any reason why this might be?' If your gut instinct is that there may be a physical condition that they aren't aware of it would be wise to gently suggest that they check it out with their doctor. Use your intuition but please be careful. With our increased sensitivity and intuition also comes responsibility.

HEALING

Healing is also referred to as 'the laying on of hands', 'faith' or 'spiritual' healing, Reiki, and many other names and practices. For most people, but not all, their journey of discovery with energy work begins with healing in some form. Either receiving it, wishing to give it, or being told that they have 'healing hands'. Laying hands on the human or animal body to comfort and relieve pain is our most natural instinct. When experiencing pain, the first thing most people do is to put their hands over the area. Touch has always been used by humans and animals instinctively to convey sincerity, warmth, comfort, love, connection, the intent to heal and to support. Premature babies are known to gain weight faster if they have physical contact. (Tactile / kinaesthetic stimulation of preterm neonates. Field, T.M., S.M. Schanberg et al 1986.) By reaching out we transfer energy. The concept behind any hands on healing is this natural intuitive action that is used to connect with another being on a subtle level.

It's been discovered that when a person isn't well, their aura changes. When the flow of their life energy is disrupted, it's believed to cause diminished function within the tissues, organs and systems of the body. This life force is also responsive to our thoughts and feelings. It's affected when we consciously or subconsciously accept negative concepts, especially about ourselves. These feelings cause damage to the correct balance of our body, mind and spirit.

Healing works by increasing the flow of energy, cleansing the meridians and raising the vibratory level of the aura. It relaxes the mind and puts the recipient in an almost meditative state that helps the body perform self-healing from within. The body will always try to heal itself but the process cannot function properly when we're sending negative thoughts to it all the time and becoming stressed. By doing this we are constantly impeding the healing process and this allows dis-ease to set in. Healing helps the body, mind and spirit connection and brings about balance.

Once aware and attuned to universal energy, we're able to consciously draw it into ourselves from the universe. Energy enters through the healer's crown chakra and passes through the upper chakras to their heart and out through their arms and hands to the recipient. It's drawn by the recipient's body to the parts that require it. The practitioner is not depleted of their own energy and is in fact receiving healing as he or she gives it.

Researchers at Stanford University, U.S. using sensitive instruments were able to measure the energy flow in the body when healers were working and verified that it enters through the crown and exits through the palms of the hands. It also seems to flow in an anti clockwise manner. Furthermore, kirlian photography has demonstrated an increase in the emanations from the hands during treatments.

The person giving the treatment cannot direct the flow of energy, and the flow will be blocked if they try to do so. Once you stop using your logical mind to work out what is going on, you will relax and may get intuitive flashes about placing your hands in particular positions.

If you feel more tingling, heat or cold in your hands than normal when giving healing, you'll know that an area needs a lot of energy. You're unlikely to know why however, unless it comes to you intuitively. Remember that in most places there are many different layers under your hands - skin, muscles, bones, organs, glands, blood vessels, lymph channels, meridians etc. The healing energy could be focussing on any of them. It could also be correcting imbalances in the auric layers around the body or the chakras, or working to release past emotions locked into cells.

The healing energy may be shifting things on a deeper level, or healing something quite different or unexpected. The priorities of the unconscious or higher self are likely to be different to those of the conscious mind. The higher self is aware of the whole pattern and the energy will be used for what is important in sorting out the whole. Clearing up symptoms may be a long way down the list. Sometimes it's not right to get rid of problems, pains or disease just yet. Perhaps we need to learn more lessons from it. It may take many healing sessions to obtain lasting relief from symptoms. If there's a long-standing condition or imbalance, many changes may have to take place before the cause of the problem is reached and the symptoms disappear. Healing gets to the root of the problem and does not suppress symptoms in the way that many drugs do, so it can seem to have a slower effect, although I have known the benefits to be significant after just one session for some people.

The effects of healing are numerous:
- It can balance energy
- It increases awareness and intuition

- It works on healing the whole person
- It amplifies the energy you have
- It works to heal at causal level of disease
- It releases stress
- It helps to release old stored negative emotions
- It increases creativity
- It strengthens and heals the aura

As a lightworker you will automatically be a healer on some level even if you don't feel that 'hands-on' is your thing. This is because the light or high level healing energy is emitted from your energy field once you have attuned to it, so you can bring about change simply by being close to a person, place or thing. However, your hands are the most common point at which you can provide a conscious flow of healing energy. Once you've learned to channel it, the energy will flow through your hands whenever you touch with the intention of healing or helping.

You can use healing energy for:
- Yourself - daily self treatments will maintain well being, reduce stress and encourage the body's natural healing abilities.
- Adults, children or babies (even in the womb) who are injured, ill or stressed, or simply want to change or grow - physically, mentally, emotionally and spiritually.
- Animals and birds
- Promoting the growth and health of plants and seeds
- Water for drinking, watering the plants or bathing.
- Food and drinks
- Healing for the Earth

If people are ill, healing can be safely used in combination with orthodox medical care and can accelerate their recuperation. It also combines well with many complementary therapies such as massage, reflexology, kiniesiology, metamorphic technique etc. and will increase their effectiveness. To be cautious, there are certain medical conditions that should be monitored by the doctor whilst someone is having a course of healing. This would include diabetes and high blood pressure and anything where they're on long-term medication or treatments.

I have heard it said that you should not do healing over broken bones. The reason for this is that it's said that healing can occur so fast that the bones can set incorrectly. However, I personally disagree. I've given healing over broken bones, as have other healers who I know and they haven't had this situation occur. I believe that the energy will aid the healing process and as it's part of our natural state of existence, it has an intelligence of its own which means that what is best for the recipient will occur. Healing can do wonders for shock and to calm someone if they've had an accident, but equally should not be used instead of standard emergency first aid. Please use your common sense in these situations, I think healing is wonderful but, if I get hit by a bus please call an ambulance first and give me healing later.

HEALING POINTS

- Firstly the term 'healing' is perhaps a slight misnomer and often misunderstood. In my opinion and experience it's a phrase which means 'the provision of universal energy to one who requires re-balancing emotionally, physically, mentally, spiritually or energetically'. On a physical level our bodies naturally find balance and harmony if at all possible so are programmed to heal themselves. Sometimes they need an extra boost of energy. Sometimes they may be considered 'ill' because of a lack of or reduced energy flow, which 'healing' can also help with.
- Secondly, once a person receives the energy boost it's up to them how their energy system utilises it depending on where they are on their own journey and how developed they are spiritually.
- Most importantly, healing is not the same as curing. Many other factors must be taken into the equation because very often the person requiring healing isn't truly ready to receive it on some level. All a healer can do is provide the energy boost. The rest is up to the person receiving it.

Healing Energy <u>A</u>

This exercise helps you to feel and channel the energy and also to send healing out to your surroundings and promote calm and peace.

- Sit comfortably either in a chair or cross-legged on the floor.
- Ensure that you have created a protective environment to work in.
- Take your awareness to either your feet (if seated) or the base of your spine (if sitting on the floor). Imagine roots extending out through this point and down deep into the earth.
- See these roots glowing with a bright white light. This is the powerful earth energy that nourishes all living things. The roots glow so bright and carry this energy all the way up to you and your contact with the ground. This wonderful energy enters your energetic system at this point and moves up through your body and along the line of the spine. Feel it as it reaches each chakra point – the base, sacral and solar plexus.
- Then once you feel the energy at the heart chakra, allow it to rest here while you take your awareness to just above the crown. Visualise a beam or funnel of pure white light coming down from the heavens. This is heavenly energy from the spirit realms. It enters your energetic body through the crown chakra and streams down through your head and neck towards your heart chakra.
- At the heart, this energy meets with the first and they become one.
- Visualise this combined energy being funnelled out through the heart chakra as a beautiful pink light that streams forth to those around you enveloping the world in a wonderful pink healing mist.
- You can channel this energy for as long as you wish, or as long as you feel comfortable doing so. It will also have a healing effect on you. You will feel calm and peaceful, connected with the universe. You may find yourself smiling, or indeed, tears rolling from your eyes. This is fine and natural.
- When you're finished visualise a small door sliding across the crown, closing your connection with the heavens (although it will never truly close). Also visualise the bright white roots turning to dark brown. Close and ground your energies.

Giving Healing

If a person needs healing for any reason you can simply place your hands on the area and get your energy flowing, or hold their hand and allow it to go where it's most needed. If you wish you can also do longer treatments that really allow the recipient to relax and benefit from the wonderful sensations of a full treatment.

Please note that working in the aura is just as powerful as physical, hands-on contact. It doesn't matter which way you do it, so always check with the recipient which they are more comfortable with. Or if you dislike working hands-on yourself, simply work in the aura, positioning your hands a few centimetres above the body. Never use direct contact within the swimwear/bikini area and remember there's no need to remove clothing in order to receive healing. It's a good idea to tell your friend that they can ask you to stop the healing at any time should they feel uncomfortable or too hot.

Full Hands-On Treatments

In Appendices A & B you will find two lists of hand positions for a full healing treatment, firstly in a seated position and then in a lying position. You may want to copy them and put them on the wall while you perform a full treatment to prompt you as to where to move your hands to. Both types of treatment can also be viewed as microworkshop videos on our website www.thepowerinyourhands.co.uk.

It's important to remember that these are not written in stone but should be used as a guide. You'll find that, with practice your intuition will start guiding your hands to certain areas or to stay at one place longer than another. Hold the hand positions for as long as you feel is needed. Trust your instincts, you or the recipient may not be able to explain them at the time but the energy always knows best. When I was doing my 2nd degree Reiki a friend of mine (who always starts a full treatment at the head) said that she didn't know why she was doing it but she was going to start my treatment at my abdomen. Two months later I was diagnosed with an ovarian cyst and had to undergo surgery - supported by Reiki throughout of course.

When you feel the energy flow stop, or if the recipient appears to become agitated (look for their feet or fingers twitching in particular) then you should finish the treatment and ground your energies. You may need to talk the recipient through the grounding process too or they could feel too spaced out.

Group Healing V
Group healing is very powerful, it is when a team of healers work together on one person at a time. In this way several hand positions can be performed at once and treatments can be performed more quickly. As a healer you can learn and develop quickly from working like this. In larger groups healers may only do two or three hand positions and one person may hold the same position for the entire session, for example, the feet or ankles. The person at the head should lead the healing, giving silent signals (such as a nod of the head) when it's time for everyone to change to the next position and when it's time to finish the session. They should also maintain physical contact with the recipient until all of the other healers have removed their hands, and then slowly remove theirs too. The process may take a little forward planning (e.g. timings and positions) and practice to feel comfortable doing it, but it's well worth it for all concerned.

The Big 'H' from 'Essential Reiki' by Diane Stein. V
I love this group healing exercise. Working on the recipient's back the team leader stands at the head with one hand on each of their shoulders. The healers at the sides alternate their hands, placing them in a column along the spine. (See the diagram on the next page.) A further healer, if there are enough, can remain at the feet. This is a powerful technique and energy can often be felt surging back and forth from head to feet. Hold the positions for as long as required or for an agreed length of time.

A similar position can be used on the front of the body with 3 or 4 healers (one at the head, one at the feet and one either side). The person to the left places one hand below the pit of the throat, the healer to the right places one hand below the breasts, the first then places their other hand below this and the second person below that. This is obviously easier on a man and hands should be positioned with care, or held in the aura, so that the recipient does not feel insecure. Again this is a very powerful technique.

THE POWER IN YOUR HANDS

The Big 'H'

Distance Healing

Believe it or not, we don't have to be with a person physically in order to pass on healing energy to them. Distance or remote healing is a practice that many healers use to help people, places and scenarios. In this way we can also send healing to the earth, plant and animal kingdom and regions of the world where there is conflict or unrest.

I believe that outside of our physical bodies we can be anywhere, and there is plenty of anecdotal evidence of distance healing being extremely effective. Equally there are many scientific trials that show that remote healing has a positive impact regardless of the belief or background of the healer or the recipient, and regardless of whether they have knowledge of it being done for them.

Some people say that healing should never be sent without the recipient's permission. This is a personal decision that each individual healer must make. Personally I disagree with this and will send healing to any person place or situation that I believe requires it. I consider that healing is no different to love and as we do not ask permission to love or care for someone we do not need to ask permission to send loving, healing thoughts. This energy will be received by the individual and processed as they wish on a subtle or energetic level. If it's appropriate and accepted it will be used for their healing, if not it will dissipate.

Distance or remote healing can be as simple as asking the universe for healing energy to be sent (something that we always do when working in development circles). For those who have done Reiki level 2 you will know that there is a specific way of using Reiki for distance work so you can follow this process. For others, try the following visualisation and the 'healing bear' exercise.

Distance Healing Visualisation:
- Sit comfortably either in a chair or cross-legged on the floor.
- Ensure that you have created a protective environment to work in.
- Take your awareness to either your feet (if seated) or the base of your spine (if sitting on the floor). Imagine roots extending out through this point and down deep into the earth.
- See these roots glowing with a bright white light. This is the powerful earth energy that nourishes all living things. The roots glow so bright and carry this energy all the way up to you and your contact with the ground. This wonderful energy enters your energetic system at this point and moves up through your

body and along the line of the spine. Feel it as it reaches each chakra point – the base, sacral and solar plexus.
- Then once you feel the energy at the heart chakra, allow it to rest here while you take your awareness to just above the crown. Visualise a beam or funnel of pure white light coming down from the heavens. This is heavenly energy from the spirit realms. It enters your energetic body through the crown chakra and streams down through your head and neck towards your heart chakra.
- At the heart this energy meets with the first and they become one.
- Visualise this combined energy being funnelled out through the heart chakra as a beautiful pink light or mist.
- Imagine the people that you wish to send healing to standing in front of you now. See them being engulfed in this gentle pink healing energy.
- Let the energy flow for as long as you wish maintaining this image. If you cannot see this in your mind's eye, mentally ask for the healing energy to be sent to each person, place or situation and then allow the energy to flow through you.
- Close and ground and thank the universe.

Healing Bear:
- A great way of sending healing is to use a representative model of the person you're sending it to - a teddy bear or small doll is perfect. (No pins are involved!)
- Give the bear or doll a name badge if you wish with the name and location of the recipient on it.
- Ask your guides and angels that they help to ensure that your healing reaches the person concerned and then simply hold it and let the energy flow. In this way you can place your hands on the specific area that requires the energy. This can also be used if for any reason you are unable to put your hands directly onto a person, perhaps they do not like to be touched, or maybe a person who has an infectious illness or who is in intensive care.
- I also find that you can use a doll or teddy to work with children who may not sit still for very long. You simply imbue the item with healing energy and ask that it be transmitted to the child while it is near to them.

Self Treatment
One of the most important elements of healing is learning to provide healing for yourself. In reality, any healing practice will act as self-treatment, but it's good for

you to take time out for you. This isn't selfish. We are each responsible for our own healing. The more we bring ourselves back to balance and wholeness, the more we will contribute to the well-being and transformation of the whole world.

I believe that self-healing is in fact a part of our own journey of spiritual development because as we channel and open to higher levels of energy, we become more enlightened, more at peace with ourselves and more at one with our true nature; that of a spiritual being, a part of the universal energy itself.

Treating yourself to some healing every day will increase your sense of self-worth and your ability to love yourself. This will help you to speak and live your truth and allow others to do the same without feeling threatened. It will enable you to give and receive more love and positive energy.

You may want to set aside time to give yourself a healing treatment, for example, when you wake up or before you go to bed at night, or as part of your meditation or relaxation practice. You can put your hands on yourself and let the energy flow into you whenever you wish. I like to place my hands on my abdomen before I go to sleep at night but you can easily work unobtrusively when other people are around by simply placing your hands on your knees, or even placing your hands together palm to palm and letting the energy flow.

You can use self-healing to:
- help you to relax when you feel stressed
- centre you when you feel scattered
- energise you when you feel drained
- calm you when you feel afraid
- focus your mind and help you find solutions to your problems
- relieve pain
- accelerate healing of wounds, infections or injuries
- improve health, gradually clearing up old illnesses
- prevent development of dis-ease
- help to release emotional wounds, limiting fears and attitudes and damaging behaviour patterns
- find new opportunities and support you in making changes

SPIRITUAL & PSYCHIC DEVELOPMENT

Connecting and channelling universal energy allows us to work on our spiritual and psychic development. It can help us to work as a medium or clairvoyant, connect with the spirit world, sense and work with the auras and chakras, learn to meditate, practise psychic development exercises and much more.

You can work on your own but it's infinitely better, and you'll develop faster, if you work in a group. In a group two things are essential, firstly rapport and harmony between the individuals and secondly an energy resource. It's necessary to have a lot of energy to facilitate your group work as spirit use it to make themselves known to us and the more physical you require this interaction to be, the more energy is needed. Physical work includes table tipping, automatic writing, object movement and manifestation. Here are two exercises to help you with these essentials:

Harmonising Exercise A
This exercise helps you to connect and harmonise as a group and should be done at the start of each session. Before doing this, don't forget to put protection in place and consciously connect with the universal energy. As a group you should sit in a circle to work at your optimum.

- Sit comfortably either in a chair or cross-legged on the floor.
- One person in the group should say the following:

"Let us blend and harmonise our energies as we sit together in circle. Let us send out a note of harmony to the person on our left by visualising a pale pink mist coming from our heart area and moving towards the heart of the person sitting on our left. As we continue to do this, become aware of receiving the same loving energy from the right. As we send and receive this, an energy circle is formed that encompasses all of us. Be aware of any changes in the atmosphere within the circle. Have a sense of oneness with the group."

- Now you're ready to do any energy work before Closing & Grounding

For Group Work As An Energy Source A
- Sit comfortably either in a chair or cross-legged on the floor.
- Ensure that you have created a protective environment to work in.

- Consciously connect and perform the harmonising exercise (p.47).
- Join hands in order to focus and build up the energy.
- Close your eyes and take your awareness to either your feet (if seated) or the base of your spine (if sitting on the floor). Imagine roots extending out through this point and down deep into the earth.
- See these roots glowing with a bright white light. This is the powerful earth energy that nourishes all living things. The roots glow so bright and carry this energy all the way up to you and your contact with the ground. This wonderful energy enters your energetic system at this point. And moves up through your body and along the line of the spine to the 'hara' just below the belly button.
- Once you feel the energy here take your awareness to a point just above the crown. Visualise a beam or funnel of pure white light coming down from the heavens. This is heavenly energy from the spirit realms. It enters your energetic body through the crown chakra and streams down through your head and neck towards your hara.
- As these two streams meet and become one at the hara, feel the energy building up - a powerful warmth may be felt.
- Become aware of the palms of your hands and the connection you have with the group. You should feel warmth or tingling as your focus encourages the hara energy to be pulled through you to your hands to be utilised for the group work.
- Maintain your contact and simply let the energy flow. You may occasionally experience different sensations such as your arms wanting to 'float' or move, or 'power surges' where your body, arms or hands shudder slightly. This is quite normal, just let the energy flow.
- You can continue to create this battery effect for as long as you wish, or as long as you feel comfortable.
- When you're finished visualise a small door sliding across the crown, closing your connection with the heavens (although it will never truly close). Also visualise the bright white roots turning to dark brown. Close and ground your energies.
- This exercise can be practised for its own sake, or you can now go on to use the build up of energy for healing, or other energy or development work (like that in The Spiritual & Psychic Development Workbook, see page 104/105).

MAGIC & MANIFESTATION

Many people shy away from the term 'magic' in fear of its association with subjects such as witchcraft, voodoo, 'the dark arts' etc. In my opinion, most of this is due to fear, ignorance and media hype. I happily use the term in lieu of other more acceptable phrases such as 'creative visualisation', manifestation, 'the law of attraction' and 'cosmic ordering'. I believe that magic is our connection with life, our oneness with the universe and everything in it. Once connected, we are able to tap into and utilise the power of the universe to assist us in achieving our dreams and desires. Used with positive intention magic is much the same as prayer.

There are rules and restrictions (although perhaps these are self-imposed by our own sense of morals and ethics). Magic should not be used to manipulate others or to go against the will of another. And always remember the age-old saying, what you give out you get back, some say threefold, so be careful!

There are in fact many elements to magic but the one I wish to focus on in this book is manifestation. When we're connected with the universe it's possible to manifest situations that we wish for, or need. Need a job after redundancy? Why not focus some universal energy on the situation? To be fair you're probably doing it in some way without thinking however, you might be focussing the wrong type of energy on the situation by worrying, stressing and wondering 'but what if...?' If you alter the way you're thinking, by using the following tips you could well be far more successful in achieving a positive outcome.

Occasionally I come across someone who has an issue with manifestation. They may think it's wrong to want to use the energy for something of a more material nature. If you're wondering about this subject, think about it this way: Healing is the conscious focussing and channelling of energy to a subject (person or ailment requiring healing) to bring about positive change. Manifestation is the conscious focussing and channelling of energy to a subject (situation requiring change, new job required, bad relationship to sort) to bring about positive change. In my opinion, there is really no difference. However, as always, you should only ever work in ways that you feel comfortable.

How to Manifest:
- What is it that you want to achieve? Write it down in as much detail as possible. If it's a job, what salary, holiday entitlement, what type of people do you wish

to work with or for, what do you want the job to do for you, do you need to feel appreciated and recognised for example? Write every aspect that you require down on your list and put a date that you wish to receive it by.

- Now place this list in an envelope and write on the front something like, 'I am so grateful for this wonderful new opportunity'. It's important to express your thanks and gratitude for the things you ask for from the universe. By doing this you are acknowledging that what you want already exists and is out there for you, you are showing your faith in the universe and affirming that it's already yours.
- Sit quietly and connect, hold the envelope and let the energy flow through you and into it.
- When you feel that you're finished, place the envelope somewhere safe. I have friends who have a manifestation box where they place all their 'orders'. This means that whenever you have a moment you can hold the box or think about it as a whole and focus energy into manifesting all of your dreams within it.
- If you work with others in a group or workshop, or have friends who do this too, you may want to ask them to help by sending positive thoughts to help you manifest what you want.
- Whenever you think about your 'order', smile and say 'thank you', have a sense of knowing that it will come, then just let the universe do its thing.
- Remember that this isn't something to do instead of going out and looking for a job or taking action to achieve what you require or want. Any positive action you take to achieve your goal will be super charged by the energy being focussed on it, so don't just sit back doing nothing and think that the universe will deliver, it still might, but it makes it harder. Think about this, the universe may deliver the perfect job, but if you're not looking at the 'recruitment' section of the paper or sending out your C.V., how are you going to know about it, let alone get an interview? All of the energy will have been wasted and you will think it hasn't worked.

BE SEEN – OR NOT!

Do you ever get days when it seems that you might just as well be invisible? Or those when you wish that you were? Well, with practice, it's possible to allow yourself to be more, or less visible to others, as you wish.

As a general rule people tend to pick up on your energy, or 'see' you more when you're more vibrant, energised and happy. You tend to be less visible if you're withdrawn and quiet. Usually people have no conscious control of this phenomena, most don't even realise that it's happening but can't work out why they're being ignored. If we take these ideas and practice consciously altering our energy fields accordingly we can take control of when and where this happens. It isn't always solely dependant on your energy but will also be affected by your physical posture. The better your posture, the more confident you will appear, and therefore, the more visible you are to others. So when it come to your energy and your physical 'presence' one cannot help but influence the other and being aware of both is necessary. Instead of working with just one element why not become fully empowered and use both your energy *and* your physicality with full awareness?

Before you start, you should be aware that being more visible will bring you a lot more attention. People will look at you more intensely because, whether they know it or not, they can sense your light shining brighter than others'. It can take some getting used to.

While I know that I'm able to make myself less visible, it still surprises me when it happens. Although not as much as it surprises anyone I speak to who hasn't noticed me being around!

You may be wondering why you would want to be able to control this. Here are some ideas:

You might want to be more visible:
- If you are presenting to or training others
- During meetings where you need to get your point across
- At events, restaurants or other occasions when you feel others may be dominating,
- When you need to get someone's attention, whether it's a waiter or someone you are attracted to.

- When you need to come across as confident and in control.

Being less visible can help you:
- If you are at an event where you feel uncomfortable
- If you see someone you really don't want to speak to
- If you feel as though you just need some time for yourself.
- If you're in a rush and don't have time to be noticed and drawn into others' conversations.

Here are some exercises to get you started:

Be Seen A
This exercise builds on the earlier exercise of expansion of your energy field to make it bigger and brighter.

- Put energetic protection in place and make your connection with the universal energy.
- Ensure that you are standing tall, engage your abdominal muscles slightly and feel the crown of your head lifting slightly upwards.

Opening – Elevate your energies
- Take your awareness back to your feet, and to the energy entering through your soles, imagine it travelling up through your legs to the base of your spine.
- At the base of the spine imagine that the energy becomes a sphere of deep red mist or light, as you visualise it, it's becoming more vibrant in colour.
- From this point a beam of energy leaves the red sphere and travels up towards the sacral area, just below the belly button. Here it forms a sphere of vibrant orange mist or light. As you focus on it, it becomes stronger in colour.
- Gradually a beam of energy leaves the orange sphere and travels up towards the solar plexus, where it forms a sphere of clear yellow. With each breath, this yellow becomes stronger and brighter.
- Once more a beam of energy leaves this sphere and continues its journey up to the heart area. Here a sphere of mist or light begins to form, which you may see as either green or pink. Focus on this area for a few breaths, allowing the energy to grow stronger and clearer and to expand.
- Gradually a beam of energy leaves the heart area and moves upwards to the

throat. Here it forms a sphere of clear blue. Once more, as you focus on this area, allow the colour to expand and increase in strength.
- Now, visualise a strand of energy leaving the throat area and linking with the third eye area, just between and slightly above the eyes. Here energy will begin to form as before. You may see this energy as either a rich indigo or violet, whichever you prefer. Concentrate on this energy and visualise it increasing in strength and energy.
- Again, a beam of light extends upwards from this area moving to the crown. As it does so, become aware of another beam of energy coming down from high above to meet the first at the crown. A sphere of pure energy begins to form in this area.

Expand your energies

- As you hold this vision for a few breaths the light grows and strengthens. The sphere becomes larger and brighter and as it does so, the beautiful pure light begins to overflow down and around you, surrounding you in this wonderful energy. It fills your aura, cleansing, balancing and strengthening it.
- The light around your physical body grows stronger and brighter. It surrounds you like a large egg shape.
- Take a deep breath in and as you do so, visualise the egg-shaped aura pulling in toward your physical body as if you are inhaling the light into your lungs.
- As you exhale slowly, breathe this light energy back into your aura and see it in your mind's eye expanding further out, brighter and clearer than before.
- Take a couple more breaths and see it extending further, maintaining its strength and brightness. You feel safe and comfortable. You feel relaxed and light.
- Now take your awareness to your feet. Lift the left one slightly off the ground and as you place it down again, imagine that you are plugging into a power socket in the earth. Feel the solidity of your connection as though you are magnetised to the ground. Now do the same with the right foot.
- Now you are ready to get out and be seen. Walk confidently and with purpose, and smile. When you meet others look into their eyes and nod, say hello or smile at them as though you are acknowledging yourself, or the divine spirit within each of them.

In time this process will become quicker to do and you will whiz through each phase getting it down to a fine art, until eventually it will seem as though you can simply flick a switch to be seen. Practice, but don't be surprised at the reaction from others, you'll get stared at a lot when you do this. People aren't used to actually seeing each other.

Be Invisible! <u>A</u>
I love doing this, but please be careful with it. If you feel that you're in a situation where you're vulnerable do not rely solely on this method, to keep you safe. Please use your common sense. Also don't be surprised if you get knocked into in busy areas as people just won't see you!

- Before doing this exercise, put energetic protection in place and connect with the universal energy. Then use the first part of the opening exercise to elevate your energies – but don't continue to the expansion.
- Take your awareness back to your feet, and to the energy entering through your soles, imagine it travelling up through your legs to the base of your spine.
- At the base of the spine imagine that the energy becomes a sphere of deep red mist or light, as you visualise it, it's becoming more vibrant in colour.
- From this point a beam of energy leaves the red sphere and travels up towards the sacral area, just below the belly button. Here it forms a sphere of vibrant orange mist or light. As you focus on it, it becomes stronger in colour.
- Gradually a beam of energy leaves the orange sphere and travels up towards the solar plexus, where it forms a sphere of clear yellow. With each breath, this yellow becomes stronger and brighter.
- Once more a beam of energy leaves this sphere and continues its journey up to the heart area. Here a sphere of mist or light begins to form, which you may see as either green or pink. Focus on this area for a few breaths allowing the energy to grow stronger and clearer and to expand.
- Gradually a beam of energy leaves the heart area and moves upwards to the throat. Here it forms a sphere of clear blue. Once more, as you focus on this area, allow the colour to expand and increase in strength.
- Now, visualise a strand of energy leaving the throat area and linking with the third eye area, just between and slightly above the eyes. Here energy will begin to form as before. You may see this energy as either a rich indigo or violet, whichever you prefer. Concentrate on this energy and visualise it increasing in strength and energy.

- Again, a beam of light extends upwards from this area moving to the crown. As it does so, become aware of another beam of energy coming down from high above to meet the first at the crown. A sphere of pure energy begins to form in this area.
- Now imagine your aura surrounding you like a large egg shape filled with beautiful white light.
- Take a deep breath in and as you do so, visualise the egg-shaped aura pulling in toward your physical body as if you are inhaling the light into your lungs. As you do so, your aura shrinks down as close to your body as you can imagine.
- As you exhale slowly, imagine you're breathing out this light but that it's transformed into tiny particles of light, much like glitter or flimsy gossamer. It fills your, now much smaller, aura changing it slightly from a solid bright white egg to an iridescent shimmering veil.
- Imagine your physical body transforming into the same light particles (as though about to be 'beamed up' in Star Trek). Take your time to visualise your whole body in this way.
- You may feel slightly weird and disconnected but this is quite normal and a good reason to only do this for short amounts of time.
- When you no longer need to be invisible please ensure that you visualise your aura back as a lovely light-filled oval shape around you and that you fully ground yourself.

OTHER THINGS YOU COULD TRY

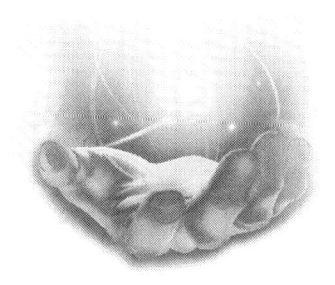

"Someday perhaps the inner light will shine forth from us, and then we'll need no other light."

Johann Wolfgang Von Goethe
(Writer, artist, theoretical physicist, biologist & polymath)

There are loads of exercises you can do to enhance your energy connection and to find the things that you're good at and drawn to do. The ones in this section will give you an idea of some of the directions you can go in with your new understanding and skills. The more you do, the more you will connect with and increase your inner light. Remember this is just the beginning, a starting point for aspiring lightworkers.

Have a read through and practise the following exercises so that you can continue to develop, find your path and fulfil your wish to connect and work with the universe. You will find more ideas and exercises in 'The Spiritual & Psychic Development Workbook – A Beginners Guide' or its accompanying 'Course Companion'. These will take you through theory and practical elements of various subjects such as working with crystals, colours, chakras, healing, dowsing and connecting with spirit. Details can be found on pages 104/105.

Looking At Auras
It's possible with practice to learn to tune into a person's aura or that of a place or object, and pick up information about it, either visually or simply by 'knowing'

or 'sensing'. Information that we may pick up could be the colours in the aura, its strength, any weak spots, imbalances or damaged areas.

'Looking at Auras' Exercise
- Working with a friend, one of you (the subject) should stand up or sit in a chair, preferably against a pale background. If this isn't possible attach a large sheet of white paper to the wall behind. (Sheets from a cheap flipchart pad are ideal.)
- The other person should be sitting opposite the subject at least five feet away. Look past the subject at the air around or above them allowing your eyes to relax and go slightly out of focus.
- You may notice the air changing around your friend, perhaps appearing thicker.
- You may begin to see the etheric aura first, like a clear glow outlining the body.
- Eventually you may start to see colours or you may sense them in some way, perhaps a colour, feeling or sensation pops into your head.
- Share what you pick up. If you're working in a group you may find that others are getting the same information as you.
- Or, you could use crayons or coloured pencils to draw what you 'see'. You can see the 'body/chakras outline' in appendix D (page 97) as a template. This can also be downloaded from the 'Readers Resources' on the website.

You can observe the auras of plants and animals for some extra practice, but take it easy, it's a different type of exercise for your eyes than they're used to so don't do too much at any one time.

Dowsing the Chakras - V
Work with one or two friends and use a pendulum for this exercise. I personally prefer to use a crystal pendulum, clear quartz is a good one to start with.
- One person (the subject) lies on their back on the floor or a couch.
- The second person holds the pendulum in the subject's aura at the feet but in line with their spine. Allow the pendulum to hang free about 1-2 inches above their physical body. From here, slowly draw the pendulum along the mid-line of the body.
- You may feel the pendulum dragging through the auric energy at certain points and it may even appear to stop. If you feel that you want to pause, then do so. The key with this exercise is to use your intuition. At the chakras it will usually

pause and either spin or make crossways movements, although sometimes it will remain still.
- If you have a third person they can observe and record the movements of the pendulum on a copy of the 'body chakras outline' in appendix D (page 97).
- If the pendulum spins it indicates that the chakra's energy is flowing well.
- However, if it spins widely, it can indicate that the chakra is too open. This may indicate that the person needs to be more protective of their energy. They may be losing energy to others or to the ether for some reason. The reasons will depend on which chakra is affected.
- If the pendulum spins but in a very small, tight circle or remains still it can indicate that the chakra is too closed. Again the reasons depend on the chakra. If you pause for a short while, the pendulum may move more as it clears and energises the chakras.
- If the pendulum criss-crosses, let it continue to do so until it begins to spin. This can take some time and indicates that there is an energy blockage. The pendulum will work to free up the blockage and allow the energy to flow as it should. Reasons for this are similar to those listed when chakras are too closed.
- Use a copy of the 'Chakra Guide' in appendix C (page 95) to analyse your results at the end.

Psychometry
In the same way that we can sense energy emanations from others and from our surroundings, we can also learn to pick them up from objects. This is known as psychometry. It could be likened to being able to feel and translate the fingerprints left by anyone who has touched an object. Objects can be 'read' like other tools such as tarot cards or used to connect with a loved one in spirit in order to receive messages for the owner.

As you hold an object in your hands you may find words or images popping into your head that have no meaning or relevance to you. It's important that you simply pass them onto the person whose object you're reading.

Psychometry Exercise
- Working with a friend, they should provide you with an item of jewellery or a personal possession.
- Before you begin ask for protection and consciously connect with universal

energy. You may also like to centre your energy.
- As you hold the item in your hands open up your energy field and focus on the energy of the object. Relax. Feel its memories, allow images to form in your mind's eye, take note of fragrances, feelings, sensations, words that pop into your head or sounds that you may hear. Say the first thing you get. Don't try to analyse it too much. What are you doing with the object? How are you handling it? That can also mean something to or represent something about the sitter. For example, twisting and turning an object in your hands could indicate that the person is restless, or feels that they are going round in circles with a problem or it may have been a familiar action of a particular loved one.
- Sit quietly for a few minutes and tell your friend what you're sensing or seeing.

When trying psychometry, whether you write down the information as you receive it and feedback to your partner later, or talk them through it straight away is up to you, but it's a good idea to keep a written record of the messages. They may be validated later by friends or family members. Your friend may have to check up on it to confirm the details or you may receive information about a future event. Remember, this skill requires practice.

Crystals
A really useful and easy method that can help to maintain the balance and increase the vibration of your energetic system is the use of crystals. Here are my tips and favourite gems for energy work:

The first thing that you should always do with a new crystal is to cleanse it, although you should find out a bit about them first as some can't be cleansed in water. Cleansing is done to shift any energy left by those who have handled the crystal before or that may have been absorbed by it from its previous surroundings. Cleansing can be done in a number of ways. It can be held in a flowing stream out in nature, or even under the tap, asking that any negative energies be washed away and recycled by the earth into positive ones. You can bury them in a pot of soil or salt (preferably rock salt), or in the garden. Or they can be left in salt water for a few hours. Alternatively, you could simply hold it in your hands asking for it to be cleansed or visualise a cleansing pure white light around it, although I'm not so keen on this method.

You should cleanse and recharge your crystals regularly. Recharging can easily be achieved by leaving them in the sunlight, moonlight or rain for a few hours (again, beware of porous crystals). Crystals love thunderstorms and seem to be especially charged up after being left outside during one.

Best crystals for energy work:
- Amethyst – for spiritual wisdom, help with meditation and working with the crown chakra.
- Clear Quartz – to cleanse and magnify your energy and for spiritual development and growth.
- Blue Kyanite – to align the chakras.
- Black kyanite – to align the chakras and ground your energies.
- Black tourmaline – big guns protection.
- Boji Stones – always in pairs, carry one on your left side, the other on your right to balance and boost your energy.
- Rose Quartz – to help balance your heart chakra.
- Sodalite – to realise and speak your truth, assists in balancing the throat chakra.

Chakra Balancing Exercise
- You will need to get a chakra set consisting of seven crystals each resonating with one of the seven major chakras, for example base – hematite, sacral – red carnelian, solar plexus – citrine, heart – rose quartz, throat – sodalite, 3rd eye – amethyst, crown – clear quartz.
- Simply lay on your back on the floor and place the relevant crystal at, or near to each chakra. For the base and crown chakras you will probably find it easier to put them on the floor above or below the chakra points as appropriate.
- Relax and meditate for a short while and see if you pick up any energetic fluctuations.
- You could try the 'Dowsing The Chakras' exercise before and after doing this to see if you notice any changes.

There are many other crystals and they can also be used in combination with energy work to enhance your abilities. So if you're drawn to crystals, I would suggest you read up on and have a play with them. I love crystal energy.

PERSONAL EMPOWERMENT

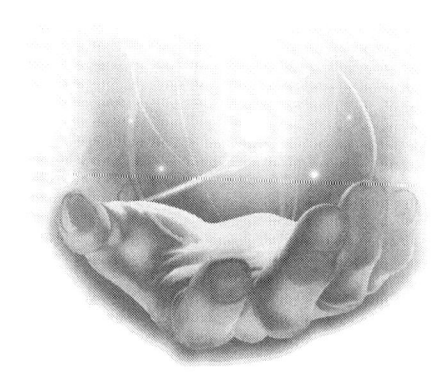

'Our deepest fear is not that we are inadequate. Our deepest fear is that we are powerful beyond measure. It is our light, not our darkness that most frightens us. We ask ourselves, Who am I to be brilliant, gorgeous, talented, fabulous? Actually, who are you not to be? You are a child of God. Your playing small does not serve the world. There is nothing enlightened about shrinking so that other people won't feel insecure around you. We are all meant to shine, as children do. We were born to make manifest the glory of God that is within us. It's not just in some of us; it's in everyone. And as we let our own light shine, we unconsciously give other people permission to do the same. As we are liberated from our own fear, our presence automatically liberates others.'

Marianne Williamson
(From her book, A Return To Love: Reflections on the Principles of A Course in Miracles)

Bringing everything together and incorporating your new outlook into everyday life can help to bring about balance and harmony. Connecting with and learning to use spiritual energy will empower and enlighten you in many ways.

IMPROVING YOUR ENERGY LEVELS

I believe that as well as ensuring our physical body is healthy, we should also ensure our energetic body is in tip-top condition. In fact, some energy workers believe that imbalance starts in the energy field and if not dealt with, eventually manifests as a physical ailment. So, it could be argued that looking after our energy system should be our first priority.

However, it matters very little which comes first as the methods that can be used to work on one will also have an affect on the other.

Our energy can be weakened or inhibited by poor diet, lack of fresh air, lack of exercise, lack of rest, illness, stress, alcohol, drugs, tobacco, negative thoughts or habits or by not protecting ourself sufficiently from external negative influences, especially when working psychically. To maintain your physical and energetic being at its best ensure that you:
- Eat a healthy balanced diet
- Take regular exercise
- Get plenty of fresh air
- Have enough rest and relaxation
- Reduce toxins in your life including alcohol, tobacco, caffeine and environmental pollution.

Other things that can help are:
- Regular meditation (including practising your visualisation skills)
- Alternative or energy therapies (reflexology, aromatherapy, Reiki or other healing methods, acupuncture, shiatsu, homeopathy, Bach flower remedies, massage, sound therapy, health kiniesiology)
- Singing, dancing, being creative
- Being you and having fun!

Other things that will be useful to address are a little harder to eliminate such as,
- Negative thought patterns
- Damaging habits
- Unhappiness
- Stress

But here's the good news, start working with energy as described in this book, and that in itself will have a positive influence on these issues. This will, in turn improve the health of your energy system. It's a win-win situation, so no excuses!

Other tips to help are:
- Use positive affirmations
- Identify the cause of stress, what your damaging habits are, or the cause of your feeling less than happy and then find ways to reduce or eliminate it

- Do more activities that make you feel positive and happy about yourself
- Smile lots!

IMPROVING YOUR LIFE

Whatever your reason for wishing to work with energy, or be a 'lightworker', you will, in the beginning underestimate the impact it can have on you. Even if you believe your mission is to assist others, you cannot help but benefit yourself, and ultimately we can only ever be responsible for our own lives anyway.

Even one of the more recognised methods of healing, the system known as 'Reiki', did not start out as such. Mikao Usui, the founder of Reiki, began by teaching students who came to him for spiritual development. The aim of his teachings was to help his students to achieve enlightenment.

Enlightenment has many definitions but the one that I prefer is, 'understanding the truth of the mind and process of existence'. Enlightenment results in liberation and freedom; we can see the 'light' of information and understanding. I certainly found that by re-connecting with universal energy, a light went on for me.

Usui and his students found that healing was an amazing side effect of the process of spiritual development and people began coming to him for healing as well. Reiki evolved to eventually become a systemised method of learning and passing on the ability to channel energy for healing. The spiritual element has generally been forgotten about.

However we work with energy, it affects us on all levels.

- Physically it helps us to relax, but also to have more energy.
- Mentally it assists in our 'letting go' and allows us to stop worrying and to focus on the moment. After all, it's only the moment that you're in at any one time that you can control, so it's only the moment you're in that is important.
- Emotionally it gives us freedom to no longer be trapped by negative feelings, and have a better understanding of ourselves and of others.
- Spiritually it helps us to raise our awareness and our consciousness, to understand our path and our lessons, to become a better person and to be the best version of ourselves that we can be.
- On an everyday basis you'll find that you walk taller and with more confidence. You'll become more noticeable to others, feel lighter on your feet, and be less affected by those around you. You'll start to find a more spiritual outlook on life and have a greater understanding and acceptance of the 'stuff' that goes on in life.

Whenever you need to you can tap into this limitless source of powerful energy to give yourself a boost. I consciously connect and use the energy on a daily basis, to boost my feeling of being alive, to walk into business situations with confidence, just before walking onto stage to speak, even when I'm out for a run to keep me going. It's not cheating, it's the essence of life, of who we are and what we're made of. It's no different to drinking water or taking vitamins. It's a free life giving, life affirming resource and it is limitless.

BE POWERFUL BEYOND MEASURE

Eventually, self-empowerment, self-awareness, self-understanding and self-acceptance are developed.

Rather than thinking that these are side-effects of helping others, I believe that helping others is the side-effect of such personal and spiritual development and I believe that this is what Usui discovered too.

Isn't it interesting that we use the words 'power' and 'light' to name this universal energy, both integral in the words, 'empowerment' and 'enlightenment'? Is that telling us something? I believe so. I love the quote used at the beginning of this chapter. Nelson Mandela used it at his inauguration speech too.

'Our deepest fear is that we are powerful beyond measure'.

The day I realised this, before I had ever read or heard this quote, it was an epiphany. I can still remember where I was. Because being so powerful, having the ability to do anything is frightening. It also means that there are no more excuses. Your life is your own to do with as you will. And you can do anything that you choose. So, tap into the universal energy system, embrace it and you will most certainly become empowered and enlightened. How far you wish to take this, how powerful you wish to become, is entirely up to you.

The Power Is In Your Hands.

APPENDICES

APPENDIX A -
HAND POSITIONS FOR A SEATED HEALING TREATMENT - V

START BY STANDING BEHIND THE RECIPIENT; PLACE YOUR HANDS IN THE FOLLOWING POSITIONS:
SHOULDERS - TO MAKE INITIAL CONTACT
TOP OF HEAD
ONE HAND ON **EACH SIDE OF THE HEAD**

MOVING SLIGHTLY TO THE SIDE OF THE RECIPIENT:
1 HAND ON **FOREHEAD**, THE OTHER ON THE **BASE OF THE SKULL**

RETURN TO STAND BEHIND THE RECIPIENT:
SHOULDERS
SIDES OF UPPER ARMS
UPPER BACK
MID BACK
LOWER BACK

MOVE TO ONE SIDE OF THE RECIPIENT & PLACE HANDS IN THEIR AURA - **1 AT THE FRONT, 1 AT THE BACK** WORKING OVER THE FOLLOWING CHAKRAS:
THROAT
HEART
SOLAR PLEXUS
SACRAL

MOVE TO STAND IN FRONT OF THE RECIPIENT:
KNEES
FRONT OF LOWER LEGS
ANKLES
FEET
BREAK YOUR CONNECTION BY STEPPING AWAY AND EITHER CLICKING YOUR FINGERS, CLAPPING YOUR HANDS, SHAKING YOUR HANDS OR BRUSHING YOUR PALMS TOGETHER A COUPLE OF TIMES.

APPENDIX B -
HAND POSITIONS FOR A HEALING TREATMENT LAYING DOWN - V

START BY STANDING BEHIND THE RECIPIENT; PLACE YOUR HANDS IN THE FOLLOWING POSITIONS:
SHOULDERS - TO MAKE INITIAL CONTACT
OVER THE EYES - IN THE AURA
TOP OF HEAD
ONE HAND ON **EACH SIDE OF THE HEAD**
BACK OF HEAD AS MUCH AS POSSIBLE AS THOUGH CUPPING THE SKULL IN YOUR PALMS
OVER THE COLLAR BONE - JUST BELOW THE THROAT

MOVING TO ONE SIDE OF THE RECIPIENT:
WORK DOWN THE FRONT OF THE BODY WITH THE HANDS IN THE AURA
COVERING THE CHEST AREA - **HEART CHAKRA**
LOWER RIB CAGE - **SOLAR PLEXUS CHAKRA**
UPPER ABDOMINAL AREA - **SACRAL CHAKRA**
LOWER ABDOMINAL AREA.
OR
IF RECIPIENT PREFERS TO LAY ON THEIR FRONT:
SHOULDERS
UPPER BACK
MID BACK
LOWER BACK

ARM NEAREST YOU - **1 HAND ON SHOULDER, 1 ON UPPER ARM**
1 HAND ON LOWER ARM, 1 ON HAND
MOVE TO THE OTHER SIDE AND **REPEAT** ON THAT ARM

PLACE ONE HAND ON OR ABOVE EACH:
THIGH
KNEES
SHIN

ANKLE
TOP OF FEET

LEFT FOOT:
1 HAND ON TOP, 1 HAND UNDERNEATH FOOT

RIGHT FOOT:
1 HAND ON TOP, 1 HAND UNDERNEATH FOOT

TO FINISH PLACE ONE HAND ON TOP OF EACH FOOT WITH THUMBS HOOKED UNDERNEATH & PLACED ON 'BUBBLING SPRING' POINT. PRESS FAIRLY FIRMLY TO BEGIN AND THEN GRADUALLY RELEASE PRESSURE AND REMOVE HANDS FROM THE RECIPIENT COMPLETELY.

BREAK YOUR CONNECTION BY STEPPING AWAY AND EITHER CLICKING YOUR FINGERS, CLAPPING YOUR HANDS, SHAKING YOUR HANDS OR BRUSHING YOUR PALMS TOGETHER A COUPLE OF TIMES.

APPENDIX C -
CHAKRA GUIDE

Base Chakra - Red
Located at the perineum, this chakra opens downwards. It connects us to the physical world, keeps us grounded and is said to be the seat of the collective unconscious. If this chakra is too open we may be overly concerned with material things, possibly self-indulgent. If this chakra is too closed we may be run down physically, have a tendency to worry too much, or feel 'away with the fairies'. Grounding work would be important to keep our feet on the ground.

Sacral Chakra - Orange
Located two fingers below the navel. It's related to our primordial emotions, security, sexuality, empowerment and creativity. If this chakra is too open we may crave a more meaningful relationship, not realising that the most important one is with ourselves. We may need to be more embracing of the miracles of nature. If this chakra is too closed we may withdraw from the attention or sensual signals from others, life may seem a bit boring, we may need to learn to express our feelings.

Solar Plexus Chakra - Yellow
Located at the diaphragm, this chakra is our power centre. It connects us to the astral body and helps us to perceive the vibrations of others. If this chakra is too open, we may be too open to the energies of others and need to learn to protect ourselves. (Folding our arms over this area if feeling uncomfortable can help prevent us from picking up negativity from others or our surroundings) If this chakra is too closed, we may be insensitive to others' energy or to our surroundings. We may need to learn to extend our awareness and be more observant.

Heart Chakra - Green (sometimes pink)
Said to be the seat of unconditional love. This chakra is related to healing, empathy and sympathy. It connects us to the spiritual aspect of others and ourselves. If this chakra is too open it's possibly as a result of constantly putting others before ourselves. A closed down heart chakra is often found in those who

do not like themselves, or find it difficult to trust or love others. We may need to learn to be kinder to and forgive ourselves.

Throat Chakra - Blue

This chakra relates to expression, communication (including listening) and inspiration. It connects us with the mental body. An overly open throat chakra is common among public speakers, or those who feel driven to communicate continually for whatever reason. A closed down throat chakra is found if we are unable to communicate our feelings with others, if we don't listen to others or fail to notice signs around us.

Third Eye or Brow Chakra – Indigo or violet

Located slightly above and between the eyes. This chakra relates to psychic perception and intuition. It's said to connect us to all levels of creation. If this chakra is too open we may be too focused on intellect and reason, try to rationalise everything and influence the thoughts of others. If this chakra is too closed we may only accept what we can actually see, be forgetful or lose our head in a crisis. In either case we may benefit from developing our intuitive and psychic side.

Crown Chakra - Violet or white

Located on the crown of the head, this chakra opens upwards. It's related to universal knowledge and connects us to the spiritual plane. The crown chakra becomes more open with spiritual advancement. It cannot be too open. The crown is always connecting us to spirit, however, if it appears small or narrow, you may wish to actively pursue a more spiritual path.

APPENDICES

APPENDIX D -
BODY / CHAKRA OUTLINE

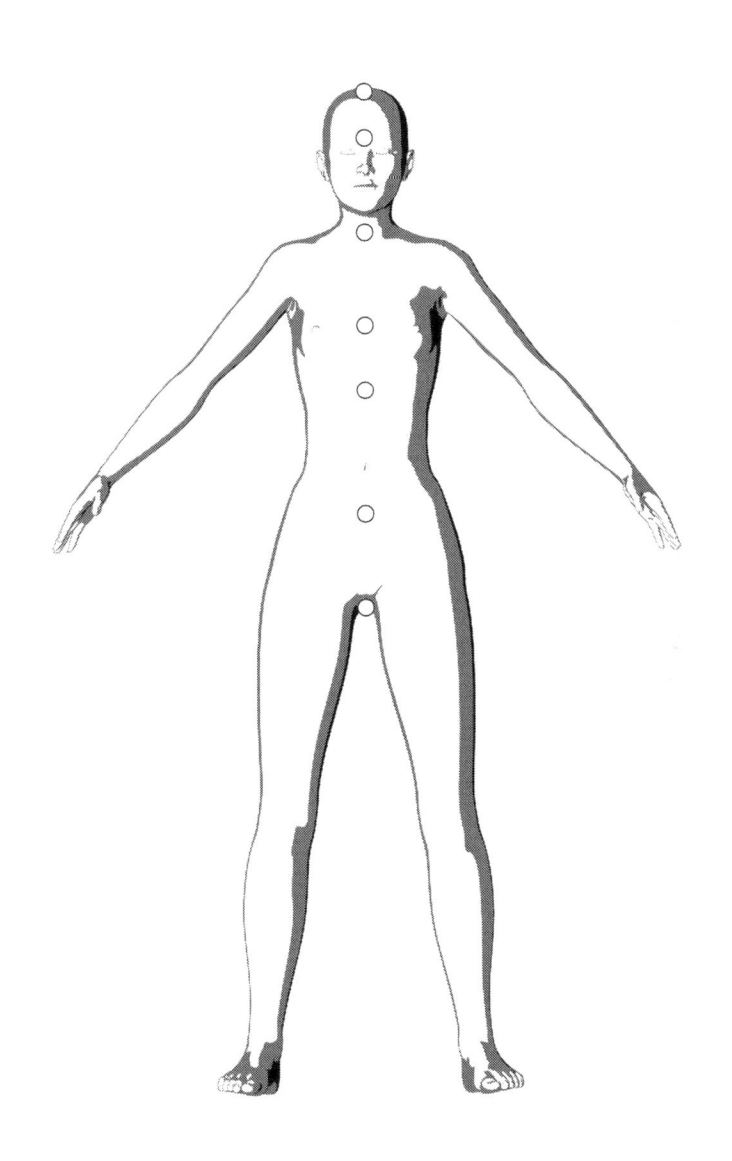

RECOMMENDED READS

To start with:
Essential Reiki - Diane Stein
The reiki sourcebook - Bronwen and Frans Stiene
The way of energy - Master Lan Kam Chuen
The Secret - Rhonda Byrne
The Power - Rhonda Byrne
The Magic - Rhonda Byrne
How to see and read the aura Ted Andrews
The field - Lynne McTaggart
Conversations with god books 1, 2 & 3 - Neil Donald Walsh
E-squared - Pam Grout

For advanced energy and spiritual philosophy:
Stalking The Wild Pendulum - Itzak Bentov
Harry Oldfield's Invisible Universe - Jane and Grant Soloman

ACKNOWLEDGEMENTS

Discovering the concept of energy was one of the biggest single life changing events I could possibly have had. So much else seemed to just fall into place once I understood the basics of it. My thanks go to:

In the beginning; my parents for being open minded enough to allow me to have healing at a young age, Sue, now with the angels but not forgotten, Marion for her workshops and crystal knowledge, My first Reiki Master, and my second Lynne Wakerly.

On the journey; Christina, Jan, Diane and all of 'Petals', and all of those who have come along to my reiki courses over the years.

For helping with this book, Jan Allgood, Gina Krupski, Vivien Leyland-Green, Denise Evans, Sara Helmsley, Andrea Allen, Jen Hawkins, Chris Smith, Michelle Lowbridge and John Leathers.

I'd also like to acknowledge Lee Kayne (in case no-one else does) and dedicate the section entitled 'Be Seen' to him...

ABOUT THE AUTHOR

About The Author

From as far back as I can remember I have seen and communicated with Spirit. Our family home had a number of ghosts, one of which was a wonderful gentle nurse from the early 1900s. Seeing, hearing and sensing ghosts, prophetic dreams and trusting my intuition and inner guidance to avoid potentially negative situations were all a part of my life from very early on. I had devoured all of Doris Stokes' books on mediumship well before I was 12. I started reading Tarot when I was 14 and also discovered a natural ability for dowsing with a pendulum. I attended courses and workshops whenever I could from the age of 18 and found a deep affinity with crystals and the native pagan culture of the British Isles. I trained as an alternative therapist and became a Reiki Master. I loved Reiki straight away and knew without a doubt that I had to teach others about it. The self-empowerment, the wonderful healing stories, and the changes that it facilitates in people are all amazing. I started running courses as soon as I could and continue to do so, seeking to make it as accessible to everyone as possible.

Over the years my psychic side became more prevalent and I also realised how empathic I was. I feel the emotions of others, the joy, the fear, and the pain. This can be difficult sometimes but I'm also able to see their potential, which is inspiring. Throughout my twenties I worked closely with friends of like mind, some much more experienced and some at a similar point to me. We discovered more and more about ourselves, our abilities and how to tap into our inner power and knowledge. We debated spiritual philosophy and universal mysteries long into the night. I continued to do card readings and dowsing but also developed other skills including psychometry and mediumship. I was invited to join a psychic development circle where I met and started working with Diane and others. I found that I was drawn to and had the ability to do rescue work. In layman's terms this is performing something like an exorcism, a horrible phrase conjuring many negative and scary images, but one that most people will understand. Basically I'm good at getting rid of unwanted and problem ghosts. A haunted antique cauldron being the first and most unusual situation that I came across.

At 30 I relocated to Shropshire I found myself with a very definite purpose. I had to share my acquired knowledge and understandings with a larger audience.

ABOUT THE AUTHOR

I was running workshops and a website for personal, spiritual and psychic development and had also started writing. Books began to take shape and I knew this was the next step for me.

My journey so far, punctuated by many paranormal experiences, has been a massive learning and development process, and I continue in this every day. I know that I'm connected to the Universe as many seeming coincidences continue to put me in front of the right person at the right time, in a better place, or out of harm's way. I don't consider myself to be special, I have simply chosen to actively pursue this avenue, to open to and connect with the Universe and to develop my own natural abilities, to ask more questions and look for more answers. I enjoy helping others to do the same.

OTHER BOOKS

Available online at www.spreadingthemagic.com

HELP! I THINK I MIGHT BE PSYCHIC
101 Frequently Asked Questions About Spiritual, Psychic & Spooky Stuff
Answered by Helen Leathers & Diane Campkin
This book is for everyone who has ever asked. "What's it all about?", "Is there life after death?", "What's it like to see a ghost?" and other virtually unanswerable questions.
Do you have fascination with or passing interest in the paranormal? Do you have a more pressing concern and don't know where to turn for the answers? Do you suspect you have a talent, a path, a dream or desire that you are not fulfilling and you really wish there was more to life?
Whether you have had supernatural experiences or not, this book will give you the basics, and a whole lot more.
This is our take on the often confusing and occasionally egotistical world of the paranormal. A reference point that's open and honest and that looks to blow away some of the cobwebs surrounding the more esoteric side of life and death, as we see it.
This book is for everyone. Do you want to know more…?
ISBN: 978-0-9558571-0-2 RRP £7.95

BRIGHT BLESSINGS
Spiritual Thoughts, Inspirational Quotes and Philosophical Observations on Life.
Helen Leathers
Ever wonder about the bigger picture and the spiritual side of life?
Do you need inspiration? Are you happy?
Do you truly know who you are and where you're heading?
This is a collection of articles, observations and quotes which aim to make you stop and think. Whether you need inspiration, a quiet moment, a focus for meditation, spiritual or philosophical advice or support, or maybe something different to do this weekend, this is the book to have within easy reach.
ISBN: ISBN: 978-0-9558571-1-9 RRP £5.95

THE SPIRITUAL & PSYCHIC DEVELOPMENT WORKBOOK
A BEGINNERS GUIDE
Helen Leathers & Diane Campkin

An introduction to the theory and practical basics of spiritual and psychic development from meditation to dowsing, card readings to working with the chakras, understanding crystals to connecting with your Spirit Guides. Do you want to increase your intuition, work with healing energy, learn how to meditate or develop your own clairvoyant abilities?

This book will facilitate the opening up to and development of your own natural spirituality and psychic skills. Essential basics, simple to understand theory and practical exercises make this a beginners guide for everyone. And there's not too many long words either.

This is the book we've been looking for for years!

ISBN: 978-0-9558571-2-6 RRP £9.95

THE ADVANCED SPIRITUAL & PSYCHIC DEVELOPMENT WORKBOOK
Helen Leathers & Diane Campkin

Building on our 'Beginners Guide' this workbook looks at the more advanced subjects within spiritual & psychic development. In an easy step-by-step process you can venture into subjects such as:

- Deep Meditation • Energy work • 3rd eye chakra development • Past lives
- Psychokinesis • Manifestation • Angelic energy • Psychic art
- Automatic writing • out of body experiences • trance mediumship.

In this workbook we want to continue to help you develop your own spiritual ethos and understanding as well as your natural psychic skills in a safe and supported way. Endeavouring to keep things as simple as possible, we provide various theories and practical exercises, include our top tips and share some personal experiences of our own.

RRP £9.95

Our range of e-books can be found in all formats at www.smashwords.com or on Amazon Kindle.

OTHER BOOKS & PRODUCTS

TWO IN-DEPTH COURSE COMPANIONS FOR WORKSHOP LEADERS OR THOSE RUNNING DEVELOPMENT CIRCLES OR GROUPS INTERESTED IN SPIRITUAL OR PSYCHIC DEVELOPMENT:

THE SPIRITUAL & PSYCHIC DEVELOPMENT WORKBOOK
A COURSE COMPANION
Helen Leathers & Diane Campkin

An in-depth course book for workshop leaders, development groups or a bunch of like-minded friends. Based on our 'Beginners Guide', the course companion is a step-by-step guide to running your own group, circle, or series of workshops on spiritual & psychic development - or just use it for yourself!
You don't have to think about it, we've done all the planning for you, a 12 part course of lessons including:
- Preparation • How to open and close meetings • Essential basics
- Easy to understand theory • Practical exercises • Handouts / worksheets
- Extra ideas and activities to complement each lesson and develop your skills further.

An essential workbook based on our experience of running groups, courses and workshops.
RRP £19.95

THE ADVANCED SPIRITUAL & PSYCHIC DEVELOPMENT WORKBOOK - A COURSE COMPANION
Helen Leathers & Diane Campkin

An in-depth coursebook for workshop leaders, development groups or like-minded friend. Based on our 'Advanced Workbook', and following on from our 'Beginners' Course Companion' this is a step-by-step guide to the more advanced subjects within spiritual & psychic development. Whether you're running your own group, circle or workshops or just using it for yourself this 'Advanced Course Companion' is an essential workbook based on our experiences of running groups, courses and workshops. Advanced subjects include:
- Deep Meditation • Energy work • 3rd eye chakra development • Past lives
- Psychokinesis • Manifestation • Angelic energy • Psychic art
- Automatic writing • out of body experiences • trance mediumship.

You don't have to think about it, we've done all the planning for you. A 12 part course of lessons including:

- Preparation • How to open and close meetings • Essential basics
- Easy to understand theory • Practical exercises • Handouts / worksheets
- Extra ideas and activities to complement each lesson and develop your skills further.
- Spiritual philosophy & discussion subjects

RRP £19.95

Our Course Companions are A4 books. When ordered from most online stores they are perfect bound (with a spine like this book). If you would prefer a spiral bound version you will find a link at www.thepsychicworkbook.com.

OTHER BOOKS & PRODUCTS

AUDIO COLLECTIONS

Available from www.spreadingthemagic.com

THE POWER IN YOUR HANDS AUDIO COLLECTION
Read by Helen
A collection of guided visualisations and development exercises taken directly from 'The Power In Your Hands' and read by the author. These tracks include energy and development work for aspiring healers, lightworkers and anyone seeking personal and spiritual growth.
- Simple physical relaxation • The breath • conscious connection
- harmonising group energy • creating an energy source as a group
- creating an energy source on your own • elevate your energy • expand your energy • close & ground

Use this audio collection to help you work through the book and connect with universal energy to rediscover your limitless power.

THE SPIRITUAL & PSYCHIC DEVELOPMENT MEDITATION COLLECTION
Read by Helen & Diane.
Available on CD and as MP3 downloads.
CD1 Essential Beginners
Suitable for use on its own or to accompany either our 'Beginners Guide' or 'Course Companion'.
Includes 'opening & protection', and 'closing & grounding' visualisations, 'Creating Your Sanctuary' PLUS a bonus track.

CD2 Individual meditations from our Course Companion Workbook Lessons 2 - 7. Includes 'Meeting Your Spirit Guide', 'Extending Your Senses' & 'Connect with the Energy of the Earth'

CD3 Individual meditations from our Course Companion Workbook Lessons 8 - 12. Includes 'Awaken Your Psychic Senses' & 'Connect With Your Totem Animal'.

THE ADVANCED SPIRITUAL & PSYCHIC DEVELOPMENT AUDIO COLLECTION
Read by Helen & Diane.
Available on CD and as MP3 downloads.
This audio collection is taken from and complements 'The Advanced Workbook' & it's 'Course Companion'. Some tracks are guided visualisations, that will help revitalise & inspire as well as assist on your spiritual & psychic development: 'Enlightenment', 'A walk down memory lane', 'Journeys through the 3rd eye', 'Meet your guardian angel', Transforming potential', 'The inner scribe', 'The garden of abundance' & 'Discover a past life'.

Other tracks are sets of meditation development exercises or processes designed with a specific goal in mind: Deeper meditation exercises - Assistance with trance mediumship - Out of body experiences exercises.

OTHER BOOKS & PRODUCTS

NEW & UNIQUE
HELEN LEATHERS'
PSYCHIC GYM
HELPING YOU TO FLEX YOUR PSYCHIC & INTUITIVE MUSCLES.

The Psychic Gym is an online course of weekly workouts.
Helen will guide you through the course with online videos, audio downloads and your own personal workbook to record your journey.

PLUS
You will receive a BONUS WORKOUT
A FREE Crystal Set
A FREE Dowsing Pendulum
& more.

If you want a personal coach to explain the basics, encourage your natural psychic and intuitive abilities and keep you on track, visit
www.thepsychicgym.co.uk

THE POWER IN YOUR HANDS

Printed in Great Britain
by Amazon